Basic Skills
FOR CHURCH
TEACHERS

DONALD L. GRIGGS

Photography by Scott Griggs

A Griggs Educational Resource
Published by
Abingdon Press
Nashville

BASIC SKILLS FOR CHURCH TEACHERS

Copyright © 1985 by Abingdon Press

Sixth Printing 1992

This book is printed on recycled, acid-free paper.

Library of Congress Cataloging in Publication Data

GRIGGS, DONALD L.
Basic skills for church teachers
(Griggs educational resources)
1. Christian education—Teaching methods.
I. Title.
BV1534.G735   1985   268′.4   84-29032

ISBN 0-687-02488-9

Page 52 is reproduced from the Revised Standard Version of the Bible published by the American Bible Society, copyrighted 1946, 1952, © 1971, 1973 by the Division of Christian Education of the National Council of Churches of Christ in the U.S.A. and is used by permission.

Page 55, reproduced from The Holy Bible, Westminster Study Edition, published by Wm. Collins & Sons, Ltd., is from the Revised Standard Version of the Bible, copyrighted 1946, 1952 © 1971, 1973 by the National Council of Churches of Christ in the U.S.A. Used by permission

The "Bethlehem" section on page 56 is from *The New Westminster Dictionary of the Bible,* edited by Henry Snyder Gehman. Copyright © MCMLXX The Westminster Press. Used by permission.

"Birth of Messiah," reproduced on page 57, is from Volume 18 of the *Layman's Bible Commentary* published by John Knox Press, *The Gospel According to Luke,* © C.D. Deans 1959. Used by permission.

The "Bethlehem" section on page 58 is from the *Analytical Concordance of the Bible* by Robert Young, published by Funk & Wagnalls in 1885.

Also on page 58, the "Bethlehem" portion taken from the *RSV Handy Concordance,* copyright © 1962 by Zondervan Publishing House, is used by permission.

Scripture quotations are from the Good News Bible, Today's English Version—Old Testament: Copyright © American Bible Society 1976, New Testament: Copyright © American Bible Society 1966, 1971, 1976.

MANUFACTURED IN THE UNITED STATES OF AMERICA

Dedicated to
Pat, Cathy, Scott, and Mark,
partners in discovering what it means
to learn and to teach

Contents

Preface

I have written this book at a time of transition in my personal and professional life. After seven very significant years at the Presbyterian School of Christian Education in Richmond, Virginia, Pat and I have returned to our home in Livermore, California.

During my years at the school, I spent a good deal of my time trying to help graduate students in Christian education develop their own teaching skills as well as the skills to enable other teachers. Each year I altered and adapted the teaching skills course, attempting to make it as focused and practical as possible. This book is another attempt to crystalize my thinking about what is basic for teaching in the church.

At present I spend most of my time writing, conducting continuing education events for pastors and educators, leading workshops for church teachers and leaders, teaching short-term courses in colleges and theological schools, and working about ten hours a month with two nearby churches. As I work with the teachers in those churches, I am again reminded of the realities of teaching in the church. Persons volunteer from a variety of motives. They bring many gifts to their teaching, as well as many needs. They have limited time available for preparation, and almost no time for training. I thought about those teachers as I was writing each chapter. I have tried to summarize what I believe is essential, and to express again in a new way my advocacy for teaching as a high priority for leaders and members of the church.

And I have tried to respond to several concerns I often hear. One pastor stated, "I am very committed to Christian education, but I feel at a loss to know how to help the church school teachers." A director of Christian education inquired, "I have been looking for a resource I can share with new teachers, as well as experienced teachers. I want something that is practical and helpful, yet at the same time grounded in solid educational theory." I have heard many church school teachers say, "Sometimes the curriculum is great, other times it is terrible, but whether it is good or not, I feel I need more than what is in the curriculum. I need something that will inspire me to teach, that will give me some good ideas, and that I can refer to through the year."

It has been my intent to address these concerns. There are many other resources that teachers will find helpful. I have identified some of them in the Helpful Books section of each chapter. However, I think this book focuses on seven specific topics not found in any other single book.

As with every other book I have written, there is a partner who serves as critic, editor, typist, and friend. Pat has helped me think through some of the critical issues of teaching in the church. Her notes in the margin have alerted me to unclear points, misstatements, and even a few points of difference. I continue to appreciate her contribution to the development of my writing projects.

Another member of the Griggs family has made a significant contribution to the appearance of this book. Our son, Scott, is a professional photographer for a commercial industrial studio in Santa Clara, California. Scott is an artist with the camera. I appreciate the good job he has done in providing illustrations for the book.

I appreciate very much the willingness of members and friends of the First Presbyterian Church in Livermore to allow themselves to be photographed and included on the following pages.

It is my hope and prayer that church teachers, educators, and pastors will find insights, encouragement, and helpful suggestions in the pages of this book. I would like to hear from any of you who have found the book helpful, who have suggestions for me to consider, or who have a different way of approaching some of the concerns I have addressed.

May God bless each one of you in your significant ministry of teaching in your church!

Donald L. Griggs
Livermore, California

Chapter One

_____

BUILDING
RELATIONSHIPS

Which do you remember best—some of the teachers you had in school and church, or some of the lessons those teachers taught? Most of us have clearer memories of particular teachers than of particular lessons. It is the impact of one person's life upon another that has the most lasting effect. We do not remember all our teachers over the years, but we do remember those who cared about us and related to us in meaningful ways. It would be worth the effort if each of us took some time to recall and reflect upon those teachers who have influenced us most and have contributed significantly to the persons we have become.

Do you remember a preschool or kindergarten teacher who calmed your fears and made you feel safe to be away from home?

Was there a grade-school teacher who showed extra patience in helping you master some difficult skills?

Did you have a Sunday School teacher who remembered your name and spoke to you personally when you met after church?

Was there a high school teacher who cared about you and knew you were capable of more than you were doing, and thus challenged you?

Did you ever have a teacher who invited just you to do something special?

Was there a teacher who was as happy as you in celebrating your accomplishment of a difficult task?

Do you remember a teacher who laughed, cried, cheered, scolded, and prayed because he or she cared so much about you and the other students?

Was there a teacher in your experience who saw potential in you that you did not see and challenged you to grow to that potential?

All these are examples of good relationships between teachers and students. As I reflect upon the many years of my pilgrimage as a learner in school and church, I can visualize those teachers who were so very important in my nurture.

As important as such relationships are, there are other dimensions to this concern. Church teachers can be very instrumental in helping students build relationships with one another, with their families, and with persons they meet in the community, as well as with God, whom they worship and serve.

Teaching As Ministry

When I read the Scriptures of the Old and New Testaments, I discover ample evidence that God's people are called to engage in the important ministry of teaching. To be persons responsible for the teaching ministry of the church is to be persons motivated and empowered to share the good news of God's mighty acts of creating, loving, and redeeming all humankind. Teachers and all who are concerned about the teaching ministry of the church could spend a very profitable time reading, studying, and interpreting some key passages that express the importance of teaching:

Never forget these commands that I am giving you today. Teach them to your children. Repeat them when you are at home and when you are away, when you are resting and when you are working. —DEUTERONOMY 6:6,7.

(Read all of Deuteronomy 6:1-9)

We will not keep them from our children; we will tell the next generation about the Lord's power and his great deeds and the wonderful things he has done. —PSALM 78:4

(Read Psalm 78:1-7)

That same day Jesus left the house and went to the lakeside, where he sat down to teach. . . . He used parables to tell them many things. —MATTHEW 13:1, 3

(Read Matthew 13:1-58)

You call me Teacher and Lord, and it is right that you do so, because that is what I am. . . . I have set an example for you, so that you will do just what I have done for you. —JOHN 13:13, 15

(Read John 13:1-20)

You know who your teachers were, and you remember that ever since you were a child, you have known the Holy Scriptures, which are able to give you the wisdom that leads to salvation through faith in Christ Jesus. —II TIMOTHY 3:14b-15

(Read II Timothy 3:10–4:5)

Go, then, to all peoples everywhere and make them my disciples; baptize them in the name of the Father, the Son, and the Holy Spirit, and teach them to obey everything I have commanded you. —MATTHEW 28:19-20

(Read Matthew 28:1-20)

All these passages, and many others, emphasize the importance of the relationships between those teaching and the ones being taught—especially the relationship of both teacher and learner to God.

There are two essential dimensions to the understanding of ministry. Ministry is serving others, responding to the needs of someone else, reaching out to others—helping, healing, caring, nurturing.

Ministry also involves acting, serving in the name of, or on the behalf of another. The church's ministry of teaching is done for the benefit of persons of all ages and circumstances in the name of Jesus, our Lord and Redeemer. Ministry is not the exclusive work of ordained clergy. It is not an optional or elective activity for Christians. All who are baptized are called to ministry in the service of others. There are many different acts of ministry: healing, helping, serving, visiting, feeding, proclaiming, befriending, as well as teaching.

Being a Christian teacher, ministering to others on behalf of God's mission, has more to do with nurturing relationships than it does with presenting a system of doctrine, offering interpretation of Scripture, or adhering to a particular curriculum. Being a teacher in the church involves a person in one of the most significant activities possible—helping persons grow in their relationships with one another, with their families and neighbors, and with their God.

The Importance of Relationships

The essence of the Christian faith is identified by words that describe aspects of relationships with God and with other persons. When we speak of love, sin, forgiveness, reconciliation, salvation, ministry, and many other important characteristics of the Christian faith, we are focusing on dimensions of our relationships with God and with

11

others. If we teach a session which includes the biblical text Matthew 18:21-35, the parable of the unforgiving servant, we will teach much more than the parable if we are able to involve the learners in reflecting on their own experience of relationships in which they received or offered forgiveness. In the course of time, we will teach even more when we are able to ask for forgiveness, or be forgiving of another, within the context of the teaching setting in which we are involved. The same will be true when we speak of loving, helping, caring, praying, serving, witnessing, believing, and all the other actions by which Christians are known. Those we teach will learn more quickly and be influenced more decisively when, in their relationships with their teacher, they experience the reality of which the teacher speaks.

Relationships form the foundation upon which the Christian community is built. Teachers play a vital role in that process of building relationships which leads to the building of Christian community. This is no easy task for the teachers of any church. There are many factors that inhibit the building of relationships and community. When participants in groups, classes, and programs attend irregularly, it is very difficult to maintain continuity. When some who are present wish they were somewhere else, it takes extra effort to motivate them to want to participate. When there are persons whose behavior, values, or attitudes are objectionable or disruptive, it is hard to relate to those persons in accepting, caring ways. And there are times when teachers are tired, disturbed, or preoccupied by factors beyond the scope of the class. While recognizing the reality of these inhibiting factors, teachers are challenged to work through those difficulties in order to engage in a ministry which strives to build relationships based upon acceptance and love. Though we will not always be successful, we seek to be faithful to the command of Jesus, "Love one another, just as I have loved you."

If you are presently a teacher or considering becoming a teacher, you are already blessed in many ways with the gifts required for building relationships. The teacher who has responded to Jesus' invitation to become a disciple and has committed his or her life to sharing the good news of the gospel with others has already fulfilled the first prerequisite for being an effective teacher. When your faith commitment as a Christian is enhanced by your caring about other persons and sharing yourself with them in meaningful ways, then you have fulfilled another important prerequisite.

In addition, each person brings to the teaching setting a unique combination of interests, abilities, and insights. Your past and present experiences in your family, school, work, church, travel, and community provide an excellent frame of reference from which to teach. Your interests in whatever areas, your abilities to do many different things, and your insights gained from a variety of sources all provide you with a vast reservoir of resources. When you identify the value of these experiences, interests, abilities, and insights and utilize them in your teaching, you fulfill a third prerequisite for doing a good job as teacher in the church. A fourth prerequisite is the willingness to spend the time and energy necessary for developing to a greater extent some of the specific skills required of a teacher. The remaining chapters of this book are devoted to helping you identify, work with, and improve some of those basic skills.

Though we live in a high-tech society symbolized by television, computers, and satellites, we fool ourselves if we think the essence of the Christian faith can be communicated by any means other than through the human being. Video tapes, computer-assisted instruction, satellite hookups may enhance the processes of communicating and teaching, but they will never be sufficient by themselves. They will never replace the teacher who is the only one who is able to speak, hear, respond, ask questions, hug, laugh, cry, and do all those other things that only a person can do. If those we teach become involved with and dependent upon high-tech instruments of communication in the routines of their lives, then they will need the benefits of human encounter with their teachers to an even greater degree.

Possibilities for Building Relationships

It is one thing to read about and agree with the importance of building relationships; it is quite different to be more specific as one tries to put into practice some of the skills that enable relationships to develop and mature. The suggestions that follow may be helpful to you as you seek to build relationships with and among those you teach.

When speaking to or about persons, use their names.

To suggest we should know those we teach by their names is to state the obvious. However, there are many times (because we forget or they have been absent) when we fail to address a person by name. To address a student by name is to speak very personally and directly to the student. When students come from a variety of neighborhoods and schools, they may see one another only on Sundays, so it is important to help them learn one another's names. When speaking to or about other teachers, the pastor, members of the staff, or church officers and members, it is very important to consistently refer to them by name. Name tags; games using names; stories told by persons about their names; polaroid photographs, with names attached, mounted on the bulletin board; rosters of names—all are devices to help you and the students remember and use everyone's name. Knowing another's name is the first step in building a relationship.

Work at being friendly.

Some educators suggest that we should never develop friendships with our students. Because we cannot be friends on an equal basis with all the students, they fear we will develop favorites and this will thwart our ability to relate to and work with the other students. However, if we do work at relating to all the students in ways that show friendliness, warmth, caring, and acceptance, we will develop relationships with many of the students that they may describe as friendship. It is not that we are seeking them to be our friends, but rather that we are presenting ourselves in such a way that the students may experience us as a friend.

Encourage cooperation, teamwork, and sharing.

In every teaching session, in any age group, there should be a balance between: (a) teachers working with the whole class, (b) students working in small groups, and (c) class members working individually. As teachers, we can foster the building of relationships when we plan activities that involve two or more persons working together and when we provide opportunities for small groups and individuals to share their work with the whole class. It would be an exception to the norm if there were no opportunity for teamwork in small groups and for sharing.

Accept the ideas and feelings that are expressed.

If we encourage students to explore, think, interpret, create, and express themselves, then it is imperative that we be open to a wide variety of their expressions. It is not necessary that we agree with everything the students say or do. We can have a different point of view, share that point of view, and at the same time be accepting of the other person's ideas, beliefs, values, or feelings. We can question, challenge, or ask for clarification of the other person's expression without necessarily rejecting or denying what the person has said or done. A good give-and-take interaction where differences are expressed provides a potential for building strong relationships.

Spend time in personal conversation.

If the class is large and a teacher is working alone, it is not possible to spend much individual time with every member of the class during each session. However, over the course of two or three months it should be possible to engage each student in a personal conversation, either before, during, or after a class session. There are many ways to reach out to students for a brief conversation: Inquire about special events in their lives, ask about members of their family, be sensitive to their moods, worries, joys, or comment on class participation, special interests, or abilities. In whatever way we connect through conversation with the persons we teach, we are facilitating the building of relationships. If your church implements team teaching so that the teacher-student ratio is low, it will be even more possible for you to have one-on-one conversations.

Share experiences outside the classroom.

Often students have a one-dimensional perception of teachers as authority figures responsible for presenting prescribed lessons. They seldom have the opportunity to experience their teachers in any role other than teacher. If you are able to make the time, you will discover many benefits from being with your students in places other than the church classroom. Visits in the home, picnics, field trips, seasonal socials, service projects, and retreats are all examples of ways teachers and students can enhance their relationship outside the classroom.

Pray for the students.

A teacher I know prays every day for each of her students and for all their families. She reports that not only does this enrich her prayer life, but she finds herself feeling much closer to her students and caring about them in a deeper way. We can offer prayers of intercession on behalf of our students, we can offer prayers of thanksgiving for them, and we can offer prayers of petition for ourselves as we seek God's guidance to be as wise, loving, and forgiving as possible. Relationships undergirded by prayer have the potential to become lasting relationships.

Communicate with and about the students.

An occasional phone call, a birthday card, a note saying they were missed when they were absent, and other tokens of appreciation and remembrance all contribute to building relationships between teachers and students. It is also possible to prepare bulletin boards, articles for church newsletters, and other displays for church gatherings that will communicate to others what the members of the class are learning about their Christian heritage and how they understand their relationship to God's family.

Many of the following chapters will focus on particular teaching skills that make a significant difference in the teaching-learning process. As important as all these skills are, there is nothing more important than that teachers of children, youth, and adults in the church be especially cognizant of the value of developing caring relationships with and among those they teach.

HELPFUL BOOKS

About Building Relationships

Brammer, Lawrence M. *The Helping Relationship.* Second Edition. Prentice-Hall, 1979.
Buber, Martin. *I and Thou.* Second Edition. Charles Scribner's Sons, 1958.
Dunn, Frank E. *The Ministering Teacher.* Judson Press, 1982.
Fenhagen, James C. *Mutual Ministry.* Seabury Press, 1977.
Rogers, Donald B. *In Praise of Learning.* Abingdon Press, 1980.
Shelp, Earl E., and Sunderland, Ronald, editors. *A Biblical Basis for Ministry.* Westminster Press, 1981.

CHECKLIST FOR TEACHERS

The following checklist is intended as a reminder of all the things you could do to work at building relationships with and among your students. No person can realistically be expected to answer each item in the affirmative every week. I would like you to see these items as goals to aim for, rather than as a measuring rod that causes you to feel guilty. Use this checklist three or four times during the year to see how you are doing in striving to accomplish some of the particular goals.

1. To what extent do I see my teaching as an important part of the ministry of the church?
   _____
   _____

2. Do I know the names of all my students?
   _____yes   _____no   _____most of them

3. Do I usually address my students by their names?
   _____yes   _____no   _____most of the time

4. What activities have I planned that provide opportunities for the students to work together and share with one another?
   _____
   _____

5. How have I shown the students that I care about them?
   _____
   _____

6. Have I usually been accepting of their ideas, feelings, and beliefs? Or have I tended to correct them or tried to change them?
   _____accepting   _____correcting

7. Have I found time for a personal conversation with each student individually at least once during the past two months?
   ____yes   ____no   ____working at it

8. What have I done to arrange for meeting or communicating with the students outside the classroom?
   _____
   _____

9. Do I regularly pray for the students?
   _____regularly   _____sometimes

10. Do I pray for myself as their teacher?
    _____regularly   _____sometimes

11. How would I describe my relationship with each of the students?
    _____
    _____

12. How would I describe the students' relationships with one another?
    _____
    _____

SUGGESTIONS FOR EDUCATION LEADERS

Though this book is written as a primer for church teachers and addressed directly to them, it is quite likely that pastors, Christian educators, education-committee chairpersons, and church school superintendents may want to use the book as a resource for teacher meetings, workshops, retreats, or other training events. Here are some suggested ways to use portions of this chapter in those settings.

1. At the beginning of the church school year, as part of a teachers' meeting, get-acquainted session, or teacher orientation, teachers could be invited to share briefly some memories of important relationships with their teachers in school or church. This activity would itself contribute to community building among the teachers.

2. In the section Teaching as Ministry, there are references to six passages of Scripture. One passage at a time could be used as a basis for a brief devotional. More time could be taken to involve the teachers in an in-depth Bible study; with the help of Bible dictionaries and commentaries, they could work at interpretation of one or more passages. As another strategy, invite each teacher to select one passage, read it, then discuss it with someone who chose the same passage. After a brief discussion, each person could meet with two or three others who discussed different passages. A discussion question could be, "What does the passage say to you about the teaching ministry of God's people and about your own ministry?"

3. The section The Importance of Relationships could be used as a basis for a discussion. Provide time for everyone to read the section, then open the discussion by asking, "What do you think about what you read? What would you add to the section?"

4. Invite persons to spend some time reflecting on their own experiences, abilities, interests, and insights that equip them to be able to share something significant with their students.

5. Provide an opportunity for teachers to discuss with one another the difficulties as well as the joys, the liabilities as well as the benefits, which they experience as teachers.

6. In the section Possibilities for Building Relationships, there are eight specific suggestions for building relationships with and among the students. Each of the suggestions could be used as is or adapted to provide the basis for discussion and goal setting. Be sure to present the eight suggestions as ideals to aim toward; avoid causing teachers to feel guilty if they do not achieve all the ideals all the time.

Chapter Two

ENCOURAGING PARTICIPATION
AND INTERACTION

I enjoy talking with church school teachers about their teaching experiences. I have often been impressed by most teachers' high level of motivation for doing a good job. A goal of many teachers is to involve students in the process of their own learning. They continually seek ways to encourage participation of students and to engage them in productive interaction with the subject matter, with one another, and with their teachers. Teachers who aim for increased participation and interaction on the part of the students know from their own experience (or from the experiences of others) that the students who are most motivated, most interested in what they are learning, and who gain most from class sessions are those who have invested the most in their learning. The students who spend time thinking, exploring, discussing, creating, responding, expressing, and questioning are the ones who will receive most from the activities the teacher has planned.

A common mistaken image of the teacher is that he or she must be the master of a subject in order to present information to students who are uninformed about the same subject. Teachers guided by this image work very hard to become knowledgeable about a subject and feel they must spend most of their time (and the students' time) controlling the class session as they present the content in as clear and understandable a way as possible. It is true that teachers need to be familiar and comfortable with the subject they are teaching, but it is not necessarily true that they must be experts. Teachers can be very effective in teaching a subject even though their knowledge of that subject is limited. *Their effectiveness is in direct proportion to the amount of involvement they plan for their students.* Students bring with them to the classroom a great deal of knowledge and experience which equips them to explore a subject with confidence. They already possess the ability to engage in a wide variety of activities as they learn about a subject.

An important task of the teacher, and a skill that can be developed, is to plan activities and to use resources that make it possible for students to participate with interest and enthusiasm. There are many specific ways to encourage purposeful participation and meaningful interaction. This chapter will explore a number of specific strategies.

The Importance of Making Choices

There are several factors that contribute to greater motivation on the part of students. Students who enjoy doing what they are doing are more motivated than those who do not enjoy what they are doing. That does not mean that teaching and learning in the church should be a continuous party with lots of fun and games. What it does mean is that students will be more motivated to participate when teachers consider what might appeal to them and then plan activities from which students will receive a degree of satisfaction. It is appropriate to ask students what they enjoy doing. Teachers will discover, through observation and feedback from students, the kinds of teaching activities that students respond to enthusiastically and that enable them to become involved with the subject matter.

Another factor that influences student motivation is being able to accomplish what the teacher, or the students themselves, intended to be accomplished. If an activity is too difficult or if not enough time is provided to complete the task, there will be a decline in motivation. Teachers should select activities appropriate for the subject, the students, and the time available so that students will gain a sense of satisfaction of having accomplished what was intended.

A third factor that affects the extent of the students' motivation is related to the matter of choices. Those students who are able to make choices about what and how they are going to learn ordinarily will be more highly motivated than those who are not given that opportunity. This does not mean that the teacher abdicates responsibility for what happens in the class session. Instead, the teacher plans with an awareness that there are a number of alternative ways to explore a subject, to respond to an issue, to use resources, and to express oneself creatively. When students interpret a passage of Scripture in their own words, they are making important choices. When they can decide from among several passages which to read and work with, they are making a choice. When they elect to express themselves visually rather than verbally, to use poetry instead of narrative, or to use photographs instead of paint, they are clearly making significant choices. The teacher continues to be responsible for providing the range of choices.

There are many different types of choices students can make as they decide how they will participate. Teachers enable students to make choices when they . . .

> . . . allow students to sit where they want.
> . . . invite students to decide with whom they will work.
> . . . ask questions for which there are a variety of answers.
> . . . plan for two or more learning centers.
> . . . offer alternative materials for responding creatively.
> . . . provide a variety of Bible resource books.
> . . . present a list of questions or tasks from which the students may select one or two.
> . . . presume that the students have the freedom to respond or not respond when called upon.
> . . . encourage students to express themselves in their own words.

These, and a multitude more, are examples of ways teachers make it possible for students to make choices and thus participate more actively and commit themselves more personally to the pursuit of their own learning.

In order for students to take seriously their opportunities to make choices and to be willing to engage in the process, there are several guidelines that teachers must bear in mind.

1. All the options that are presented must be valid, so that whatever choice the student makes is acceptable.

2. When students have made decisions, their choices must be respected and accepted. It is possible to discuss the choice but not in a way that would question the student's right to make the choice.

3. Students need to be helped to follow through and be responsible for the choices they make.

4. Teachers should always ask, "What are some other ways to do it?"

5. Teachers should feel free to supplement printed curriculum by providing additional or alternative options when the given lesson plans are limited.

The Importance of Questions

Questions may be the most valuable resource available to the teacher for guiding students to explore concepts and to express their ideas, values, and beliefs. Effective questions contribute significantly to increasing the participation and interaction of the students. Teachers can ask questions of a whole class or of an individual. Questions can be written on a worksheet, newsprint, or transparency to guide students' exploration. Students can state their own questions to invite responses from the teacher, other students, or even of themselves.

There are at least a dozen ways to utilize questions in various parts of the class session. Questions may be used to . . .

 . . . introduce a new subject.
 . . . discuss a familiar subject.
 . . . review a subject studied earlier.
 . . . interpret a biblical passage.
 . . . relate a biblical passage to personal experience.
 . . . evaluate a film or other resource.
 . . . motivate further research on a subject.
 . . . brainstorm solutions to a problem.
 . . . interview a resource person.
 . . . consider alternative actions.
 . . . clarify personal values.
 . . . explore commitments and beliefs.

Just as there are many ways to use questions, there are several different types of questions. Here we will explore three distinct types: fact questions, inquiry questions, and personalized questions.

We are all familiar with questions that ask students to remember specific information. This type of question focuses on facts, and the answers are either right or wrong. *Fact*

questions are very limited in their ability to provoke exploration or discussion. When teachers ask too many fact questions, students may feel as though they are taking a verbal test. In my observations I have noticed that most teachers spend too much time asking fact questions. It is not surprising that they are disappointed when the students do not show interest and enthusiasm for the subject. Although facts and information related to any subject are very important in providing background for the study, it is not necessary to deal with that information by asking a lot of fact questions. Some examples of questions that focus on facts related to the prophet Amos:

> Where did Amos live?
> What did Amos do in Tekoa?
> When Amos proclaimed the Word of the Lord, where did he do it?
> What are some of the sociopolitical issues Amos addressed?
> What was the name of the priest who told Amos to leave Bethel?

Notice that those questions would not generate very much discussion and interaction. There is a second type of question which invites students to think, reflect, analyze, and interpret a subject. These questions emphasize inquiry and have many possible appropriate answers. *Inquiry questions*, by their nature, prompt discussion and encourage students to become involved with the subject. Since persons are accustomed to being asked fact questions with right or wrong answers, teachers need to help the students become comfortable with expressing themselves freely. One way to set the stage is to preface the question with such phrases as "Why do you suppose . . . ?" "What are your thoughts about . . . ?" "What are some examples of . . . ?" "Let's think a minute about why . . . ?" Notice that each of these phrases suggests the possibility of more than one correct answer. Here are some examples of questions that will encourage inquiry and interpretation on the part of students:

Why do you suppose Amos went to Bethel to proclaim the Word of the Lord?

Of the things Amos said, which do you think was most offensive to the religious leaders? Why?

Of the issues Amos addressed, which do you think are still relevant, needing to be addressed today?

Who are some persons today who function in the role of a prophet like Amos?

In addition to the above two general types of questions, there is still a third type which also encourages student involvement and discussion in a more personal way. *Personalized questions* are very open-ended. Because persons are speaking out of their own experience and relating the subject to their own lives, there is no way they could give a "wrong" answer. Even though teachers will be accepting of the students' responses, it is possible to probe a little—to ask the students to clarify what they have said, give reasons for their comments, or expand their responses. These are some examples of questions that would encourage the students to relate the subject of Amos to their own lives:

If you had been Amos, and Amaziah had told you to leave Bethel, what response might you have made?

Tell about some times when you spoke up for what you thought was God's will and were criticized for it.

About what issue in today's society would you like to speak out?

How would you express what you believe to be "the Word of the Lord" as you address that issue?

Possibilities for Encouraging Participation and Interaction

In the last two sections we explored the importance of choices and questions as a basis for greater involvement of the students in the teaching and learning activities of the class session. Some suggestions and examples that teachers will find helpful in working with their students were given. There are a number of other specific possibilities for increasing student participation and interaction. Each of the following possibilities is described briefly and is suggestive of much more that you may want to consider and practice.

22

EXAMPLES OF QUESTIONS AND STUDENT PARTICIPATION

(BASED ON THE SUBJECT AMOS)

——— LESS INVOLVEMENT ———————————————— MORE INVOLVEMENT ———

Fact Questions	Inquiry Questions	Personalized Questions
Where did Amos live?	Why do you suppose Amos went to Bethel to proclaim the Word of the Lord?	If you had been Amos, and Amaziah had told you to leave Bethel, what response might you have made?
What did Amos do in Tekoa?	Of the things Amos said, which do you think was most offensive to the religious leaders? Why?	Tell about some times when you spoke up for what you thought was God's will, and were criticized for it.
When Amos proclaimed the Word of the Lord, where did he do it?	Of the issues Amos addressed, which do you think are still relevant, needing to be addressed today?	About what issue in today's society would you like to speak out?
What are some of the sociopolitical issues Amos addressed?	Who are some persons today who function in the role of a prophet like Amos?	How would you express what you believe to be "the Word of the Lord" as you address that issue?
What was the name of the priest who told Amos to leave Bethel?		

It is important to include all three types of questions. In order to reflect and analyze, students need to know the answers to fact questions. In order to apply subject matter to their own lives and answer personalized questions, the students must first know the facts and be able to analyze them. Because it is harder to create questions that cause students to analyze or to apply subject matter to themselves (as in personalized questions), most teachers ask too many fact questions and too few questions that fall into the other categories.

Make the subject interesting.

Students are much more likely to want to become involved in a class session that appeals to their curiosity or stimulates their imagination. With an intriguing question or a reference to a current trend or fad, by introducing a popular personality or controversial issue, or by posing a complex dilemma, teachers will encourage students to become involved more quickly in the subject of the day's session. Teachers also will make a subject interesting when they show their own enthusiasm for what is being discussed. A teacher's interest and enthusiasm have a way of being contagious.

Relate the subject to the students' own experiences.

If the subject is significant and is appropriate to the age group being taught, then there is usually a connecting link between the subject and the students' own life experiences. The feelings, thoughts, hopes, and beliefs of biblical persons, as well as those of persons throughout history, are not unlike those of persons today. The context is different, the world situation is markedly different, but the personal and interpersonal dynamics are quite similar. Teachers will be very helpful when they invite students to identify with and see similarities and differences in the persons, events, and issues of biblical times and their own personal present time.

Invite students to explore their own questions.

Everyone has questions about many, many topics. Children ask questions before they are able to give answers. Wise older adults continue to ask questions. Questions can be as simple as asking for a brief definition of a word such as *faith*, or as complex as seeking personal meaning for the same word. Rather than always being the one to ask questions or give answers, it is possible for the teacher to provide opportunities for students to ask, explore, and answer their own questions. When persons can state their own questions, it is more likely that they will be motivated to pursue those same questions. Teachers who call forth questions from their students must also be willing to accept those questions as they are stated. If the teacher has a particular question in mind, it is permissible to include that question among the students' questions. In order to search for answers to the questions they have posed, it is very important that students have access to resources that will enable them to be successful in their search.

Give clear and concise directions.

Teachers seeking to enhance the involvement of their students in the class session must design strategies that facilitate maximum student participation. This means that instead of making extended presentations of subject matter, teachers will plan for activities that engage students in their own explorations and expressions of issues, ideas, beliefs, and feelings. In order for students to become meaningfully involved and gain satisfaction from their involvement in teacher-planned activities, they must receive clear, specific, sequential directions that they can follow without difficulty or confusion.

Here are some general principles to keep in mind when giving directions:

1. Think through the complete process of the activity to determine exactly what a student must know in order to be successful with the activity.

2. Consider the skills, resources, and time necessary to accomplish the activity.

3. Divide the activity into its several separate steps or parts, and give directions one step at a time.

4. Write a statement of directions for each step, beginning each statement with action words: *read, use, listen to, find, select, list, write.*

5. Keep directions clear, simple, and concise.

6. If the activity is unfamiliar, provide an opportunity for students to experiment and practice.

7. Printed or projected directions are usually more helpful than verbal directions.

8. When preparing participants to respond creatively to a filmstrip, song, story, poem, or scripture passage, it is best to give the directions in a written form prior to presenting the resource itself. In this way there will be no interruption between the experience of the resource and the creative response to it.

25

Plan for sufficient time.

One factor must be considered when involving students in a variety of participatory activities: It always takes much more time for the students to work their own way through a subject than for the teacher to present the same subject verbally. The tendency is to underestimate the amount of time it will take students to accomplish a task. Even though lesson plans in teachers' manuals usually suggest the amount of time needed for an activity, the estimate is not always correct. There are no rules or charts I know of to advise teachers how much time their students will need for various activities. Each student works at his or her own pace, and each will need a different amount of time for the same task. Students feel frustrated if they are rushed or do not have enough time to complete what they started. Teachers are frustrated when they feel they could cover much more of the subject in the same amount of time by presenting it verbally. But keep in mind that in the end, the students will be much more motivated when they do some of the work for themselves, and they will learn much more as a result of their own first-hand experience with the subject. The best advice for the teacher is to relax, be patient, be flexible, keep the larger goals in mind, and enjoy the time of interaction with the students.

Offer praise and encouragement.

A very significant factor that influences the degree of participation by students is the amount of praise and encouragement they receive from the teacher. Students need to know that their teachers care about what and how they are doing, that their teachers care personally about them. Praise should not be given without reason, but should refer to something specific. Students feel praised and encouraged when the teacher . . .

  . . . smiles in approval.

  . . . inquires with interest about what they are doing.

  . . . incorporates their work into another part of the session.

  . . . speaks about what they have done with enthusiasm.

  . . . shares the product of their work with others.

  . . . says, "I like that," "You have done well," "That is a good start," or "Thank you."

Expressing appreciation for what students have said, done, asked, or shared always provides a tremendous incentive and contributes to the building of relationships with students, as well as encouraging them to participate actively in the class session.

HELPFUL BOOKS

About Encouraging Participation and Interaction

Hunter, Elizabeth. *Encounter in the Classroom.* Holt, Rinehart & Winston, 1972.

Knowles, Malcolm, and Knowles, Hulda. *Introduction to Group Dynamics.* Revised Edition. Follett Publishing Co., 1972.

Little, Sara. *Learning Together in the Christian Fellowship.* John Knox Press, 1956.

Sanders, Norris M. *Classroom Questions, What Kinds?* Harper & Row, 1966.

Turner, Nathan W. *Effective Leadership in Small Groups.* Judson Press, 1977.

CHECKLIST FOR TEACHERS

1. In a 45 to 60-minute class session, what percentage of the time am I doing most of the work, compared to the amount of time the students are actively involved in their own work?

    _____%teacher   _____%students

2. How many choices, and what kinds of choices do the students make in a typical session?

    _____

    _____

    _____

    _____

3. Have I offered a variety of choices, so that both the verbally oriented students and the more visually oriented ones have a choice that will be of interest?

    _____almost always   _____usually   _____not at all

4. To what extent am I accepting and affirming of the ways students choose to express themselves?

    _____

    _____

    _____

    _____

5. What kinds of questions do I ask most often?

    ____fact questions   ____inquiry questions   ____personalized questions

6. Have I been conscious of asking questions that will encourage inquiry and personal application?_____

    _____

7. Am I usually interested in and enthusiastic about what I am teaching?

    _____

    _____

    _____

    _____

8. Have I related the subject of our study to the interests and experiences of the students?

    _____

    _____

    _____

    _____

9. Are the students occasionally encouraged to ask, explore, and answer their own questions?

    ____yes   ____no

10. How have I been doing in giving directions?

    ——Students follow directions easily.

    ——Students need to have directions clarified.

    ——Students cannot remember the whole sequence of directions.

    ——Students do not follow the directions.

11. Has each student received some personal word of praise and encouragement from me in the past two or three sessions?

    ——all students   ——most students   ——few students

SUGGESTIONS FOR EDUCATION LEADERS

1. As part of a briefing session with an individual teacher or team of teachers, or as part of a larger training session, teachers could be guided to review three or four of their most recent lesson plans. They could look specifically for one or more of the following:

How many activities were planned in which the students were able to make choices?

What kinds of questions were planned and used?

What directions were written out to guide the students?

How much time was allowed for various activities?

After reviewing the lesson plans, teachers should be helped to make some personal judgments about what they have discovered. They could work with plans for future lessons in order to make improvements in areas where they feel something lacking.

2. In the section The Importance of Questions, each of the three types of questions is described. As part of a meeting or workshop, the teachers could read that brief section or it could be presented by the leader. After they become familiar with the unique features of the three types, the teachers could practice writing questions of each type and/or preparing questions of each type for the next session or two.

3. Divide the teachers into small groups, according to the grade levels they teach. Guide them in considering a sample lesson from the teacher's manual and in a process of brainstorming to suggest a wide variety of additional choices the students could be invited to make in that session.

4. Engage the teachers in the process of writing directions for typical activities that they could plan for their students. Teachers can exchange their written directions with one another to give helpful feedback and critique.

5. Invite teachers to recall and share times when they were students and the teachers they remember. Focus on the times they felt most motivated and involved, their opportunities to make choices, and/or activities they enjoyed.

Chapter Three

PLANNING
FOR TEACHING
WITH CURRICULUM

Teachers may recognize their work with students as being an important part of the whole ministry of the church. Teachers may greatly desire that their students become actively and purposefully involved in the class sessions. Such perceptions and desires, as important as they are, do not translate easily into effective and satisfying experiences. In addition to having a strong commitment to teaching and a desire to do the best job possible, teachers need to develop some very specific skills in using a particular curriculum and developing a series of lesson plans. Teachers' experiences of teaching will be influenced significantly by the way they plan for lessons and use the curriculum.

Most persons who volunteer to teach in the church are already very busy with family, vocational, community, recreational, and church interests and responsibilities. There are very few who have the luxury of a great deal of time each week to plan their church school lessons. Many teachers would like the curriculum to be so well-structured and easy to use that they do not need to spend much time reading it and figuring out what to do on Sunday morning. Teachers with these desires are quite often frustrated. It is not like a frozen dinner, which just needs to be put in the microwave for a few minutes before it is ready for consumption. Curriculum is more like the cookbook, with recipes that suggest various options, list all the ingredients necessary, and give directions regarding sequence, time, temperature, and so on. Obviously, since it takes more time to prepare a meal from a recipe than from a prepackaged dinner, so also it takes more time to prepare a good lesson that will be appreciated by those with whom it will be shared. Just as most meals that are specially prepared are more tasty, more attractive, and more appropriate to the occasion, so lessons that are carefully prepared are more likely to appeal to the needs, interests, and abilities of the students.

While I recognize the limited amount of time available for preparing session plans, I also believe that teaching in the church is of such a high priority that it deserves as high a level of commitment of time, energy, and personal resourcefulness as teachers are able to give. Teaching in the church is not a leisure-time activity; it is not something we do after other tasks are accomplished. Teaching is central to the church's ministry with persons of all ages and circumstances.

31

Though preparing to teach involves commitment of time and energy, I am convinced that specific principles, procedures, and strategies can be developed and utilized to help teachers do their planning more efficiently and effectively. This chapter, as well as several that follow, seeks to present some very specific suggestions to assist in planning to teach with curriculum.

Ten Steps in Planning

Planning involves both a perspective and a process. By *perspective* I mean that teachers need to be able to view clearly the task that needs to be done—to see the goals in the distance and visualize the steps needed in order to complete the task and accomplish the goals. If you focus only on the task (to plan and teach a lesson for 45 minutes, with 15 students, on a subject that is not well understood), it is possible to become very frustrated, and even immobilized. If you focus only on the goals (to share the heritage of the Christian faith with students, to help them become believers and disciples, faithful to Jesus as Lord and Savior), it is possible to become overwhelmed by the magnitude of what is expected. To relieve these feelings of being frustrated and overwhelmed, it is necessary to gain some sense of the smaller steps that must be taken for effective planning in order to achieve those goals.

Planning also involves a *process*. There are first steps, next steps, and concluding steps, which lead in a logical sequence to the desired result of a helpful lesson plan. There are some steps in a process that are absolutely essential, and there are others that are more optional. There is no one absolutely reliable sequence of steps that guarantees successful planning and teaching; there are many helpful variations to the planning process. Each curriculum plan with its teachers' manuals, each experienced teacher, each author of a book such as this, will present a particular approach. Teachers should not change their own process each time they encounter a different curriculum, teacher, or author. It is important, however, that they adopt, use, revise, and continue to use a planning process that works for them.

Contained in the steps that follow is my conception of a process for planning. The process is developed in greater detail in other resources I have written. Even though I may present this process in a way that seems definite and dogmatic, I am quite aware that many variations are possible. There are times when situations require that I alter the steps of the process, and other times when I abandon it altogether. These steps are like the scales in learning to play the piano; once you have mastered them, you are equipped to improvise.

Step One: Consider important factors.

There are a number of important factors that influence the shape and content of the lesson plan. The amount of *time* determines the number and type of activities. The number of *students* influences whether you work in small groups, with individuals, or with the whole group. The *space* where the class meets and the *furnishing* of that space will either enhance or inhibit various elements of your plan. The *equipment* and *resources* available either make it possible or prevent you from doing some of the activities suggested in the teacher's manual. The *abilities* and *interests* of the students, as well as those of the teacher, determine whether or not activities will work. The *season of the year* influences how you go about planning. There is no printed curriculum that can anticipate all the circumstances in order to deal with all the above factors. The situation in which you find yourself and your students is one of a kind. As the teacher in this situation, you must consider the factors and respond to them personally in ways that enhance your planning for your students.

Step Two: Prepare yourself personally.

Whether this is step two, step one, or the last step is not as important as that this step be included in the planning process. Personal preparation includes *reading*. Because of the limited number of pages of a teacher's manual, there is usually not enough background information for you to feel that you are knowledgeable about the subject you will be teaching.

Read and reread the recommended Bible passages.

Read the appropriate articles or chapters in Bible resource books (commentaries, dictionaries, atlases, concordances, and word books). Even spending a half-hour with a Bible dictionary, reading the brief articles related to the key concepts of the lesson, will help you feel much more confident with the subject.

Read teaching activities resource books. One or two good books with suggested activities related to the subject would provide you with ideas for additional or alternative activities if those in the teacher's manual are not adequate.

Read about the age group you are teaching, about educational theory, and about other topics or skill areas related to Christian education.

Of course, you cannot follow through on all these things to read for each session. However, over the course of a year or two or three, you will find yourself being continually inspired, nurtured, and equipped for your ministry as a teacher if you spend some time reading additional resources.

Another aspect of personal preparation is prayer. Pray for guidance and support for yourself. Pray for your teacher colleagues. Pray for the students you are teaching now, as well as those you taught last year. Pray for the church's total ministry of education, the staff, pastor, church educator, and others. Some teachers find that reading/praying, guided by a devotional book, helps to focus their prayers and to maintain the discipline of prayer. Some practice another discipline by writing prayers in a journal, along with the other entries. A collection of personally written prayers becomes an invaluable resource that can be referred to again and again.

Step Three: Read the curriculum.

There is no substitute for reading the curriculum carefully and thoroughly. Most teacher's manuals usually have the following characteristics: (a) They include outlines for thirteen session plans for one quarter of the year. (b) The session plans are organized in two to four units of three or more sessions each. (c) Each session plan contains information about

34

the subject of the session, suggestions for teaching activities, and recommendations for structuring the lesson. (d) There are often general articles, suggestions for alternative activities, resources, and/or directions for doing particular projects.

When you receive a new teacher's manual, turn first to the table of contents and look at the outline of the lessons in order to get a quick overview of the quarter. It is helpful to read the introductions or general background paragraphs of all lessons in the whole quarter to gain a sense of the relation of the individual lessons to one another, to the unit, and to the theme for the quarter.

After gaining this overview, skim all the lessons, looking especially for activities and resources that will require advanced planning. You may need to order some special supplies or materials, or reserve a filmstrip from a resource center, or recruit a helper or two for a special project. With this advance preparation taken care of, you are now ready to focus on the first session of the first unit. Read the whole unit. Then carefully reread the session for the coming week. Write in the margins. Make notes. Do whatever is helpful to begin to get the lesson clearly in focus. As you read the curriculum, note where you have questions, where you need additional background information or help, where you plan to adapt or rearrange. If you are able to do this reading of the curriculum before you start planning a particular lesson, you will find that the next steps will be accomplished much more quickly and satisfactorily.

Step Four: Identify the main idea.

For each session there is a main idea that summarizes what is intended to be communicated to the students in that session. You find clues about the main idea in (a) the title of the unit of the session; (b) the primary biblical text for the session; (c) a paragraph, column, or brief article that provides background information for the teacher; and (d) the content of the session plan. The author of the curriculum has a very clear understanding of the main idea of the session. As the teacher, you need to identify for yourself, in your own words, your understanding of the main idea. Complete this statement: "In this session I would like to share with the students the meaning of . . . ." Write a paragraph that expresses what you believe is important to communicate to the students. Incorporate ideas from the curriculum, from your own experience and knowledge, and from other resources that help you understand the subject of the session. As you write the paragraph, be sure to relate it to the present social setting and life experiences of the students. You will find that if you write out your own main idea for the session, you will have a much clearer focus as you begin to develop the rest of the lesson plan. Here is an example of a main idea for a session that focuses on Moses at the time of God's call to him in Midian:

> In this session I would like to share with the students the meaning of God's call to Moses. Moses was born as a Hebrew and raised as a prince in Egypt. After being an advocate for the Hebrew slaves, Moses fled to Midian. Moses' life represented many different roles when he was called by God to leave Midian. He struggled with the responsibilities of these various roles as he decided whether or not to return to Egypt to work for the freedom of the Hebrews. We today are called by God to serve God and people, and we struggle with the way we should respond to God's call.

35

Step Five: Determine the objectives.

Whether it is stated explicitly or not, the authors of all curriculum have in mind the things they intend for the students to accomplish during the session. These intentions may be stated as purposes, aims, goals, desired outcomes, or objectives. Sometimes the intentions are implied, rather than stated. I prefer to speak of these intentions as *objectives*. Objectives describe, as specifically as possible, what the teacher plans for the students to be able to accomplish by the end of the session that they could not accomplish at the beginning. Goals are very important, but they are more general and more appropriate for a whole year, or even a whole lifetime, than for one session. You can write an objective by completing this statement: "At the end of the session the students will be able to . . . ." Objectives are written in such a way that they describe the actions of the students.

There are different types or levels of objectives. At the lowest level students will be able to: name, list, recall, or find—these actions are basic and simple. In another level, or type, of objective, students will be able to: interpret, express, distinguish, or illustrate. At a still higher level of involvement, students will be able to: decide, affirm, act, or practice. As you write objectives for your students for each session, be sure to use words that describe actions of the students that you can hear or see, and to include actions that represent several levels of involvement.

There are several important reasons for writing objectives: (a) They provide a focus for your planning. (b) Your selection of activities and resources will be purposeful. (c) You will have a basis for evaluating whether you and the students have accomplished what you intended. It will take a little time to write several objectives for a session, but you will find that the rest of the planning goes much more quickly.

Step Six: Select teaching activities.

Once you have identified the main idea and have determined the objectives for the session, you are ready for the more interesting part of the planning process: considering various teaching activities and selecting those that would be appropriate for the session. Teaching activities are the heart of the lesson plan. It is by means of these that the main idea is communicated to the students and the objectives are accomplished. There are many types of teaching activities: presenting, reading, interacting, creating, audio visual, writing, and so on. And there are literally hundreds of variations on each type of activity.

The teacher's manual will suggest a variety of activities appropriate to the subject of the session, and often these activities are sufficient. However, there are many times when you will need to adapt or supplement the recommended activities. The number of students present, the time allotted, the availability of materials, the interests of the students, the resourcefulness of the teacher—all influence the selection of activities. Teachers should be willing to adapt and/or supplement the activities suggested in the teacher's manual so that the lesson plan presented to the students will be especially relevant and appropriate for them. There are several criteria that should be considered:

1. Does the activity engage the students in a purposeful, involving way?

2. Does the activity provide opportunities for the students to make choices and express themselves freely?

3. Are a variety of activities planned so that students with different skills and interests will all be motivated to participate?

4. Does the activity encourage dealing with the subject in depth and with enthusiasm?

5. Does the activity help the students relate the subject to their own life situations?

6. Can the activity be accomplished in the time available?

Step Seven: Utilize resources.

In order to involve students in most of the activities planned, it is necessary to use a variety of resources. Resources can be as simple as pencils and paper, as sophisticated as computers and video recorders, and as personalized as a guest speaker. Though a computer or video recorder may be fascinating and popular with the students, it is quite possible that using pencil and paper to write a dialogue between Moses and an imaginary newspaper reporter would be more effective in helping the student identify personally with Moses.

Resources are as important for teachers and students in a church school session as pots, pans, stove, silverware, plates, glasses, table, and chairs are necessary for a family to enjoy a meal together. It is not a question of whether to plan to use resources in teaching, but rather which resources are to be used. Resources should never be used as gimmicks for their own sake, nor should they be used just to fill time or keep the students busy—that would be a misuse. Teachers should plan carefully and intentionally for the resources they and their students will use. Several criteria would help teachers select and utilize resources:

1. Does the resource enhance the students' learning and involvement with the subject?

2. Has the teacher practiced with the resource so as to be confident in its use?

3. Will the students be successful in using the resource to explore a subject or to express themselves?

4. Is the resource integrated as a part of the whole lesson so that it does not stand out in an obtrusive way?

5. Has the resource been introduced clearly, utilized effectively, and followed up purposefully?

6. Have a variety of resources been used over a period of time?

Step Eight: Develop a teaching strategy.

So far we have dealt with four important elements of a lesson plan (main idea, objectives, activities, and resources). We have dealt with them separately. In order to have a teachable lesson plan, all the elements must be integrated into a teaching strategy, a purposeful plan which brings together all the factors that influence the content and form of the lesson plan. It is important to begin the planning process with that outline as a primary reference point. However, it is equally important for the teacher to have in mind the structure of a typical lesson plan which can be used in harmony with, or as an alternative to the one presented in the teacher's manual. When teachers have in mind a reliable structure that they can use easily and effectively, then no matter what is presented in the teacher's manual or what is present in the teaching situation, the teacher will be able to do an effective job of planning. This is the structure with which I begin my planning:

Opening—I try very hard to devise an opening that . . .
   . . . invites the students to want to participate.
   . . . introduces the subject, or main idea, in an interesting way.
   . . . relates the subject to experiences familiar to the students.
   . . . calls upon the students to make some choices.

The opening can be as brief as two minutes or as long as ten minutes. The opening is the time when many students will decide whether they are pleased to be there or not.

Sample
LESSON PLANNING WORKSHEET

Date_____   Time Available_____

Unit Title_____
Session Title_____
Key Bible Passage(s)_____
_____

Main Idea: In this session I would like to share with the students the meaning of:
_____
_____
_____

Objectives: At the end of the session the students should be able to:

1. _____
2. _____
3. _____
4. _____

Time	Activity	Resources
	Opening:	
	Presenting:	
	Exploring:	
	Responding:	
	Closing:	

Presenting—Through one or another of many possible activities, teachers need to present information about the subject in an interesting, challenging format. The teacher can tell a story, pose questions, read Scripture, project a filmstrip, present a brief lecture, or carry out any one of many possible activities to share the necessary information with the students.

Exploring—Once the students have the information they need and the directions to pursue a task, they are ready to spend some time exploring the subject individually or in small groups. It is in the process of exploring a subject that students begin to invest themselves in their study. Exploring activities involve students with questions, issues, tasks, resources, and each other, so that they become equipped to offer their own interpretations, judgments, or conclusions.

Responding—In this aspect of the teaching strategy, students are encouraged to express for themselves what they think, feel, believe, and value. Responding activities help students relate the subject to their own life experiences. It is in these activities that teachers are able to discern whether or not the students are accomplishing the objectives intended for that session.

Closing—It is important to close the session in a way that summarizes some of the key elements of the whole process. Closing activities can consist of a brief prayer, a song or hymn, responses to a good question, the sharing of the results of creative expression, or the completion of an open-ended statement.

Step Nine: Use a planning worksheet.

I have found that by outlining all the elements of my lesson plan on a planning worksheet, I will have, on one or two sheets of paper, almost everything I need to serve as a guide while I am teaching. It is best for teachers to complete the parts of the worksheet in their own words. In this way, they will feel much more confident during the course of the session. The worksheet on page 39 includes all the necessary elements; however, there is not enough space to write everything that will be needed. Instead of duplicating the worksheet as it is presented here, it would be best to spread the elements out over two pages so there will be enough space for material related to most sessions.

Step Ten: Evaluate what you have done.

One way to learn from your experience and to improve your skills as a teacher is to evaluate each session as soon afterward as possible. In the process of evaluating your work you will be able to identify the strengths of the session so as to build upon them, as well as recognize the weaknesses in order to change and improve. There are several ways you could conduct regular or periodic evaluations of the sessions you have planned and taught.

1. Review the lesson plan to see if what actually happened corresponded with what you intended.

2. Focus on the objectives to see whether the students did accomplish what you hoped they would.

3. Use a portable tape recorder to record a portion or all of a session, and then listen to it, to hear what you actually say as you teach.

4. Focus on one specific aspect of the teaching process to try to analyze how well that part was accomplished. For instance, focus on asking questions, giving directions, making a presentation, telling a story, responding to students, giving choices, and so on.

5. Invite a trusted friend or respected teacher to sit in and observe your teaching. Give the observer a copy of the lesson plan and tell him or her the points you would like some help with, so that the observation will be focused and purposeful.

Summary

In this chapter we have reviewed ten important steps in the planning process. I would not be surprised if these ten steps seem a little overwhelming to new teachers. There are many decisions to make and much time involved if the steps are taken seriously. I sympathize with those feelings of anxiety, but I am also quite sure that if new teachers use these steps as a basis for their planning, and work with them conscientiously, they will discover before long that the steps can be taken more easily and naturally without stumbling. If you are an experienced teacher, you may want to use the ten steps outlined here as a basis for comparison, evaluation, and reflection on the planning process you have developed for yourself. Whether you are experienced or inexperienced, don't try to master all ten steps at once. Give yourself time and be patient as you continue to build upon the strengths and gifts you bring to the ministry of teaching in your church.

HELPFUL BOOKS

About Planning for Teaching with Curriculum

Bowman, Locke E., Jr. *Essential Skills for Good Teaching*. National Teacher Education Project, 1974.
Duckert, Mary. *Help! I'm a Sunday School Teacher*. Westminster Press, 1977.
Griggs, Donald L. *Teaching Teachers to Teach*. Abingdon Press, 1974.
Griggs, Donald L. *Planning for Teaching in the Church*. Revised and Expanded. Judson Press, 1985.
Rusbuldt, Richard E. *Basic Teacher Skills*. Judson Press, 1981.
Washburn, John. *Teaching Strategy: A Simulation Game*. National Teacher Education Project, 1972.

CHECKLIST FOR TEACHERS

1. How much time do I usually spend each week planning for teaching?
   ___less than an hour   ___one to two hours
   ___three to five hours   ___more than five hours

2. Is this usually enough time?
   ___yes   ___no

3. What would I need to do in order to have more time available for planning?
   _____
   _____

4. How many of the ten steps do I usually include in my own planning?
   _____

5. With which of the ten steps would I like some help?_____
   _____

6. Do I skim the whole teacher's manual to get an overview of the lessons for the quarter?
   ___yes   ___no   ___sometimes

7. Do I usually write out in my own words the main idea and objectives for each lesson?
   ___yes   ___no   ___sometimes

8. Have I supplemented the suggestions for activities and resources in the teacher's manual with my own ideas?
   ___yes   ___no   ___sometimes   ___I need help with this.

9. How do the five parts of a lesson plan suggested in this chapter compare with the suggestions in the teacher's manual?
   ___quite similar   ___quite different

10. Would the Lesson Planning Worksheet be helpful to me as a format to guide my own planning?
    ___yes   ___no   ___I am not sure.

SUGGESTIONS FOR EDUCATION LEADERS

1. In conversations with individual teachers or in a group meeting, it would be appropriate to talk about . . .

    . . . how much time it takes to plan for teaching.

    . . . ways they manage their time to have time for planning.

    . . . their feelings about the conflict between the time needed and the time available.

    . . . the conflicting demands upon their time and how they set priorities.

2. Each of the ten steps in planning could be developed as a one to two-hour workshop. The workshops could be offered over a period of a year or two, so that teachers would be able to work on those aspects of the planning process with which they feel they need some help.

3. The Lesson Planning Worksheet could be presented as it is (enlarged to two pages) or adapted so that all the teachers use the same planning format and process. In a workshop or teacher-meeting setting, each teacher brings one or two lesson plans to share and to receive as well as offer critique. A permanent file can be developed for each class so that copies of the curriculum, lesson plans, activity sheets, and so on are filed, in order to be available for the next person who teaches the same material. What a great help it would be not to have to start from scratch with each new lesson!

4. One or two of the resources suggested in the Helpful Books section of this chapter could be selected in order to focus on one or more of the ten steps. In a workshop or at a teachers' meeting, the particular steps can be worked with in more depth so that teachers have time to practice some of the procedures and skills related to the chosen steps.

5. A church educator, church school superintendent, or experienced teacher can plan a sample lesson that incorporates as many of the ten steps as is practical. After the sample lesson is presented to a group of teachers there should be sufficient time to reflect on the elements of the planning process that are included. It would be especially helpful to duplicate copies of the lesson plan so that all persons who participate would have a sample to refer to as they develop their own lesson plans.

Chapter Four

DEVELOPING
BIBLE SKILLS

The Bible is the basis upon which all curriculum is developed for use by teachers and students in the church. Virtually every teacher's manual and student workbook features biblical passages, stories, events, and persons. I have surveyed a variety of curriculum and have noticed that many editors and authors seem to assume that teachers and students, especially teachers, already know how to use the Bible and Bible study resources. It may be that most teachers are familiar with some of the content of the Bible. However, many teachers feel they are not adequately equipped to use the Bible skillfully for their own preparation in teaching or to use it effectively with students. This chapter will present some brief helpful suggestions for activities and resources to develop skills in studying and teaching the Bible.

In two previous chapters I emphasized the importance of encouraging students to participate actively in class sessions and of including exploring and responding activities in the teaching strategy. Active participation in these activities, with biblical materials as the primary focus, requires that teachers and students develop skills that will enable them to work with the Bible in appropriate and effective ways. Learning from the Bible requires more than just reading biblical passages, remembering them, and having a good discussion. Learning from the Bible depends upon using resources within the Bible itself as well as other study tools that help uncover the setting, the meaning, and the application of the biblical texts.

One of the goals of Christian education is to equip Christians to be able to read and use the Bible for themselves. It is not enough to depend upon pastors and teachers to present what they think is important to know and believe about the Bible. Every Christian has the right and the responsibility to be able to read the Bible and to discern what is perceived to be God's Word for his or her own life. In order to fulfill this responsibility there must be intentional, continued effort by teachers to instill the basic skills necessary for reading, interpreting, and applying the biblical teachings. When Christians are able to relate to the Bible with understanding and commitment, it is possible that the Bible may then truly become for them the living Word of God.

I have used the word *Bible* in the generic sense, without any reference to a particular translation or version. There are several factors to consider when deciding which Bible to use with various classes and groups.

1. With younger students who have limited reading skills and are just being introduced to the Bible, it is important to use a translation they can read comfortably. An excellent translation is the Good News Bible, The Bible in Today's English Version, published by the American Bible Society.

2. In their first personal, serious study of the Bible, it is best for all the students to use the same edition of the same translation, so that page numbers are identical in each copy.

3. For any age students, contemporary translations will be more helpful than paraphrased editions or outmoded translations.

4. With youths and adults, it is quite appropriate to use a wide variety of translations and versions. Such a variety will enable them to compare translations as they seek to understand the meaning of a passage.

Even if in a year's time the curriculum does not include session plans that introduce, review, or utilize the basic Bible skills outlined below, it is possible for a teacher to supplement some of the session plans throughout the year to include some practice in these skills.

Skills in Using the Bible Itself

This chapter focuses mainly on Bible skills, as opposed to Bible information or knowledge. There are other books, as well as church curriculum, which deal primarily with Bible information and knowledge. Actually, the content of the Bible and the way persons apply that content to their own faith and life experiences, are ultimately more important than the skills. However, mastering basic Bible skills makes it possible to work and live with the Bible.

Finding Bible Passages

A basic necessary skill is the ability to find Bible passages. No other book is as complex as the Bible, with two main sections (Old and New Testaments), sixty-six smaller "books" in the whole volume, and chapters and verses that subdivide each book. Add to this complexity of structure the strange-sounding, hard-to-pronounce titles of many of the books, and you can appreciate the difficulty young readers might have in trying to find passages or stories. Even adult readers who might be new Christians or unfamiliar with the Bible have difficulty trying to find their way through the Bible. It is the teachers of all age groups who have the best opportunity to help readers develop the skill of finding Bible passages. Here are some guidelines I have found helpful as I work with students of various ages.

1. *Introduce the Bible as a special book.* It is a special book in two ways: (a) For Christians, as the Word of God, it has special authority for faith and life. (b) It is also organized differently from any other book. Spend some time talking with students about the uniqueness of the Bible as the Word of God. Also, spend some time just turning pages and looking at the distinctive features of the Bible as a book.

Title—The word *Bible* comes from the Greek word *biblia*, which is plural and means *books*. The word was translated to become singular. But the Bible is more than a book. It is more like a collection of books in a small library.

Old and New Testaments—*Testament* is a translation of the word *covenant*. The Bible focuses on the covenant God made with Israel through Moses (the old covenant), which was fulfilled in the life, death, and resurrection of Jesus (the new covenant).

Books—There are thirty-nine books, or parts, of the Old Testament. The names of these books are all translations from the Hebrew language in which the whole Old Testament was written. In the New Testament there are twenty-seven books, with titles that are all translations from Greek, the original language of the New Testament.

Types of Books—In any library the collection of books includes various types of literature. In the Bible there are books of law, poetry, history, letters, prophecy, gospels, and other types.

Chapters and Verses—Prior to the thirteenth century, the books of the Bible had no chapter divisions. In 1226 the Archbishop of Canterbury, Stephen Langton, worked at dividing each book of the Bible into numbered chapters. It was not until 1551 that a French printer further divided the chapters into verses.

It is not necessary to spend a lot of time dealing with this information, but it is important for readers to be able to use the Bible successfully. Unless the teacher has resources available for the students to find the above information for themselves, it would be best to share the information directly.

2. *Use the table of contents.* For some reason, persons (mostly adults) seem to feel guilty about having to turn to the table of contents at the front of the Bible in order to find the page number for a particular book. I think they feel guilty because they presume that all the others have memorized the order of the Bible books and know where to find what they are looking for. I would always encourage younger students, as well as older ones, to turn to the table of contents for the page number of a book if they are not sure where to find it. It is very hard to find the books of Joel or Ruth or Haggai by flipping through the pages, because they are such short books. It is quicker and easier to turn to the table of contents.

3. *Practice finding books.* Persons will discover that with practice, they will be able to find most of the books without having to use the table of contents. The more they practice finding books, the more familiar they will become with their location. This practice needs to be accompanied by the awareness that often various types of books are together: The books of law are the first five in the Old Testament; the books of poetry are in the middle; the books of the lesser prophets are toward the end of the Old Testament.

It is not enough to memorize the books in their correct order. I found that when I memorized the names of the books, I often had to go through the whole list to locate the one I was looking for. It is better to use learning devices such as cards, blocks of wood, or small matchboxes with the names of the books printed on them so that students can sort, arrange, and work with the correct order. With practice, games, and simple devices, students will become familiar with the order of the books so they can usually find what they are looking for without too much difficulty.

4. *Learn the abbreviations of the book titles.* In the front of each Bible, often as a part of or near the table of contents, there is a list of the abbreviations used to designate each book. It is very necessary to learn the abbreviations in order to use footnotes, cross references, Bible dictionaries, concordances, or commentaries. In all these study resources, abbreviations are used more often than the complete names of the books. Matching games can be devised to help persons become familiar with the abbreviations. From two to four letters are used for the abbreviations. Some good examples: Ps. = Psalms; Jer. = Jeremiah; Mk. = Mark; Phil. = Philippians; Phlm. = Philemon.

5. *Master the chapter and verse references.* For new readers of the Bible this is a very important skill. Most references to chapters and verses follow a standard form. Let's use Gen. 1:1-8 as an example. Notice the abbreviation for the book Genesis (Gen.),

followed by the number 1, which refers to chapter one of Genesis. The chapter number is followed by a colon or, in some references, a period. The colon separates the chapter number from the verse numbers—in our example, the verses are one to eight inclusive. The hyphen between one and eight indicates that all the verses one through eight are part of the reference. Sometimes references suggest other combinations of chapters and verses:

Gen. 1–2, Genesis, *chapters* one through two inclusive.

Gen. 1:1–2:4, Genesis, chapter one, verse one, through chapter two, verse four.

Gen. 1:1-5, 14-19, Genesis, chapter one, and two sets of verses in that same chapter.

There are times when a verse is exceptionally long and the reference includes only part of the verse; there are other times when the break between verses does not match the break in the syntax of a sentence. In those instances a part of a verse may be identified by a letter, such as Gen. 2:4*b*. This refers to Genesis, chapter two, the second part of verse four. There is one caution to keep in mind. In many Bibles you will not find the number for the first verse at the beginning of each chapter. The chapter number is in large bold-face type, whereas the verse number is not present in any printed form.

Using chapter and verse references is another of the basic skills taken for granted by many editors, authors, and teachers. However, it is a skill that needs to be introduced, practiced, reinforced, and reviewed when students are working on developing skills for reading the Bible and finding Bible passages.

6. *Develop guidelines and strategies for working with basic skills.* In the above five sections we have introduced basic skills to help teachers and students to find passages in the Bible. Teachers, because of their greater experience with books, dictionaries, research, and so on, will be able to master these skills without much difficulty. Young readers and new older readers of the Bible may need help from their teachers to master the same skills. There are a number of guidelines and strategies teachers should follow as they work with students on these skills:

Make a game of the process—not a competitive, win-lose game, but a fun game.

Develop devices—worksheets, puzzles, and other resources—to assist the students in learning the skills.

Allow time for finding passages, completing tasks, and working with resources. Take the pressure off the students so that they feel comfortable working at their own pace.

Practice, review, and practice again, so that the skills involved in finding passages become a natural part of the students' use of the Bible.

Never cause a student to feel embarrassed or guilty when trying to find a Bible passage. Be patient and helpful to enable mastery of the skill and make learning possible.

Reading with Comprehension

When I was a child, I remember a Sunday school teacher who would ask all us students to take turns reading. Every Sunday she would divide the verses of a whole passage by as many students as were present so that each of us read the same number of verses. I remember being more concerned about whether I would be able to pronounce all the strange words correctly, than about trying to understand what my classmates and I were reading. The teacher would ask questions after we read the passage, and I felt bad because I could not answer the questions. I was sure the teacher thought we were all dumb. As I reflect upon those childhood experiences, I could now give that teacher some clues to help the students read with comprehension. Following are some ways to help students read the Bible so that they understand something of what they are reading.

1. Many young readers, especially those in grades two to five, love to read aloud. This is a new skill they are developing, so in spite of difficult words, many of them want to read aloud. They are very motivated when they receive their new Bibles and are disappointed when the teacher does all the reading. Although this is not true of all, the teacher can respond to the needs and abilities of children by selecting passages that do not have so many difficult words, or the teacher can read the more difficult parts. Another strategy would be to identify the difficult words ahead of time, talk about their meanings, and repeat the words several times in order to practice correct pronunciation.

2. Instead of taking turns around the circle, reading a few verses at a time, students can be invited ahead of time to volunteer. In that way, they have an opportunity to practice and to ask for help with difficult words.

3. When anyone is reading aloud, those who are listening will be helped considerably if they have identical copies of the text to follow. There should be enough copies of the same translation of the Bible available so that all students in the class can read for themselves. When students listen to a good reader who pronounces all the words correctly and uses appropriate emphases, they are able to begin to understand the words as they read them.

4. Reading silently is a good approach for some readers. When reading silently and independently, they can read at their own pace. The problem is that the poorer readers will have difficulty completing the assignment satisfactorily. The teacher needs to become aware of the reading abilities of the students in order to know which ones will require more time or assistance.

5. One of the most helpful things a teacher can do to increase the comprehension of the students in their own reading, or when listening to someone else, is to identify ahead of time the purpose for reading or listening. Teachers can provide a question or two (no more than two) so that as students are reading or listening they will be looking for answers to the question. Or the students can be instructed to look for something specific. By being alerted ahead of time to look for something, the students will be able to read or listen much more actively and purposefully. Afterward, it is very important to follow up by discussing, or responding in some other way to what they have discovered from their reading or listening, prompted by the prior directions from the teacher.

6. Earlier we discussed the fact that questions have the potential to increase the active participation of students. The same would be true in reading if the students were invited to write one or more questions based upon the material. The questions can be used by the students to guide their own personal exploration, or by the teacher and other students as a basis for sharing information or discussion.

7. More experienced readers will find their comprehension increased if, as they are reading from the Bible, they use a Bible dictionary to help them understand difficult or strange words. A Bible dictionary provides more than definitions of words. It provides brief articles or essays which give a lot of important background information related to key words. In addition, some Bibles have a word list, a glossary, or an abbreviated concordance.

Clearly these suggestions take a lot of time and are not appropriate for all teachers and readers every time they study the Bible. However, when teachers are planning teaching strategies that intentionally aim toward increasing their students' understanding, these suggestions should be considered in order to utilize one or more that might be helpful.

Using the Footnotes

Often readers ignore the footnotes at the bottoms of the pages when they are reading the Bible. I suspect that most of us have an aversion to reading the fine print of any document, and the Bible is no exception. However, the footnotes in the Bible can provide important background information and textual reference notes that will help one's understanding of words, verses, or longer passages. To provide a sample set of footnotes, we have reproduced a page from a Bible in the Revised Standard Version. There are several things to consider when looking at the list of seven footnotes on this sample page.

1. "Other ancient authorities" is not a reference to ancient experts or scholars, but to ancient manuscripts. There are many ancient manuscripts, which are all copies of other manuscripts that were unearthed and deciphered to provide the basis upon which biblical scholars and translators make their judgments as to how the text should be written. What we have in the body of the text may be seen as the "majority report," and what is in the footnote, the "minority report."

2. Notice that the meanings of some verses are affected when you either add or omit the words that are based upon "other ancient authorities." To add *fasting* to *prayer*, as in footnote "j," does alter the meaning of the text to some extent.

3. Footnotes "1" and "m" provide the literal translations from the Greek. What appears in the body of the text is more accurate in terms of the meaning in English and will be better understood by the readers.

4. Without footnote "n" the reader would never have an explanation for the omission of verses 44 and 46 from the text.

Reading footnotes is not the most critical skill to be mastered, but it is a skill that, when exercised, does increase one's understanding of the text. Teachers of older youth and adults should plan occasional activities that utilize footnotes when they contribute to interpreting the biblical text.

Using Cross-reference Notes

Whereas footnotes help the reader understand something of the text itself, cross-reference notes direct the reader to other places in the Bible where a particular verse or passage with identical or similar wording appears. In the reproduced copy of the page from the Gospel of Mark you will notice there are twenty-one cross references. It is not surprising that there are many cross references on most pages of the four Gospels, since the authors used common sources as the basis for their writing. Reviewing the sample page, you will notice that the material in Mark 9:49-50 is repeated in both Matthew and Luke, whereas 10:1-12 appears elsewhere only in Matthew. By checking the cross-reference for 10:4, you are able to find, in Deuteronomy 24:1-4, the source of the quotation from Moses which the Pharisees used to answer Jesus' question. Cross-reference notes are especially useful when searching for connecting links between the Old and New Testaments. If you look up the cross references for Psalm 22, you will discover a significant connection between that familiar psalm of lament and the passion narrative of Jesus.

Skills with Bible Study Resources

In the previous major section we focused on reading the Bible itself and using the built-in resources that are included in most editions. The focus of this section will be upon other resources available to assist teachers and students in their study of the Bible—study Bibles, dictionaries, commentaries, concordances, atlases, and other books.

by the hand and lifted him up, and he arose. 28And when he had entered the house, his disciples asked him privately, "Why could we not cast it out?" 29And he said to them, "This kind cannot be driven out by anything but prayer."*l*

30 They went on from there and passed through Galilee. And he would not have any one know it; 31for he was teaching his disciples, saying to them, "The Son of man will be delivered into the hands of men, and they will kill him; and when he is killed, after three days he will rise." 32But they did not understand the saying, and they were afraid to ask him.

33 And they came to Caper'na-um; and when he was in the house he asked them, "What were you discussing on the way?" 34But they were silent; for on the way they had discussed with one another who was the greatest. 35And he sat down and called the twelve; and he said to them, "If any one would be first, he must be last of all and servant of all." 36And he took a child, and put him in the midst of them; and taking him in his arms, he said to them, 37"Whoever receives one such child in my name receives me; and whoever receives me, receives not me but him who sent me."

38 John said to him, "Teacher, we saw a man casting out demons in your name,*k* and we forbade him, because he was not following us." 39But Jesus said, "Do not forbid him; for no one who does a mighty work in my name will be able soon after to speak evil of me. 40For he that is not against us is for us. 41For truly, I say to you, whoever gives you a cup of water to drink because you bear the name of Christ, will by no means lose his reward.

42 "Whoever causes one of these little ones who believe in me to sin,*l* it would be better for him if a great millstone were hung round his neck and he were thrown into the sea. 43And if your hand causes you to sin,*l* cut it off; it is better

for you to enter life maimed than with two hands to go to hell,*m* to the unquenchable fire,*n* 45And if your foot causes you to sin,*l* cut it off; it is better for you to enter life lame than with two feet to be thrown into hell.*m,n* 47And if your eye causes you to sin,*l* pluck it out; it is better for you to enter the kingdom of God with one eye than with two eyes to be thrown into hell,*m* 48where their worm does not die, and the fire is not quenched. 49For every one will be salted with fire.*o* 50Salt is good; but if the salt has lost its saltness, how will you season it? Have salt in yourselves, and be at peace with one another."

10 And he left there and went to the region of Judea and beyond the Jordan, and crowds gathered to him again; and again, as his custom was, he taught them.

2 And Pharisees came up and in order to test him asked, "Is it lawful for a man to divorce his wife?" 3He answered them, "What did Moses command you?" 4They said, "Moses allowed a man to write a certificate of divorce, and to put her away." 5But Jesus said to them, "For your hardness of heart he wrote you this commandment. 6But from the beginning of creation, 'God made them male and female.' 7'For this reason a man shall leave his father and mother and be joined to his wife,*p* 8and the two shall become one flesh.' So they are no longer two but one flesh. 9What therefore God has joined together, let not man put asunder."

10 And in the house the disciples asked him again about this matter. 11And he said to them, "Whoever divorces his wife and marries another, commits adultery against her; 12and if she divorces her husband and marries another, she commits adultery."

13 And they were bringing children to him, that he might touch them; and

---

l Other ancient authorities add *and fasting*   *k* Other ancient authorities add *who does not follow us*
l Greek *stumble*   *m* Greek *Gehenna*
n Verses 44 and 46 (which are identical with verse 48) are omitted by the best ancient authorities
o Other ancient authorities add *and every sacrifice will be salted with salt*
p Other ancient authorities omit *and be joined to his wife*

[handwritten right margin: } seven footnotes]

9.30-32: Mt 17.22-23; Lk 9.43-45.   9.31: Mk 8.31; 10.33.   9.32: Jn 12.16.
9.33-37: Mt 18.1-5; Lk 9.46-48.   9.34: Lk 22.24.
9.35: Mk 10.43-44; Mt 20.26-27; 23.11; Lk 22.26.   9.36: Mk 10.16.
9.37: Mt 10.40; Lk 10.16; Jn 12.44; 13.20.
9.38-40: Lk 9.49-50; 11.23; Mt 12.30; Num 11.27-29.   9.41: Mt 10.42.
9.42-48: Mt 18.6-9; 5.29-30; Lk 17.1-2.   9.48: Is 66.24.   9.49-50: Mt 5.13; Lk 14.34-35.
9.50: Col 4.6; 1 Thess 5.13.   10.1-12: Mt 19.1-9.   10.1: Lk 9.51; Jn 10.40; 11.7.   10.4: Deut 24.1-4
10.6: Gen 1.27; 5.2.   10.7-8: Gen 2.24.   10.11: Mt 5.32; Lk 16.18; 1 Cor 7.10-11; Rom 7.2-3.
10.13-16: Mt 19.13-15; 18.3; Lk 18.15-17.

[handwritten right margin: } twenty-one cross-reference notes]

You will recall the importance of encouraging students to become actively involved in their own studies. If they are to engage in productive Bible study in which they explore meanings of passages, they will need sufficient resources to enable them to do it for themselves. These should be available in a church library so that teachers and students can check them out when needed. It is important to purchase multiple copies of a variety of key volumes, so that when resources are used in the classroom each student will be able to choose from among several. There should also be several types or levels of resources in order to accommodate the differing needs and abilities of students at all age levels.

I can anticipate a negative response to my recommendation to purchase quantities of these very expensive resources: "We hardly have enough money in the Christian education budget for curriculum. We could never afford to buy what you recommend." I know that church budgets are limited, but it is not necessary to purchase the whole shopping list of recommended books in one year, nor must the funds come solely from the church budget. There are a number of ways to secure additional quality resources for the church library.

First of all, it is important to set the increasing of the collection of resources as a priority. If a church determines that it is important to have Bible study resources available, then ways can be devised to accomplish that goal. Resources for studying the Bible are as essential to church teachers and students as are resources for preparing and serving a church dinner. Each choir member has a copy of the music for one or two anthems every Sunday—such resources are essential for doing a good job. The same is true for teachers and students. They need sufficient resources to do their job well.

After determining that purchasing resources is a goal or priority, it is necessary to develop a strategy to accomplish that goal. Here are some possible strategies:

1. Invite church members to give a Bible study resource book to the church library for Christmas. Publish a complete list of desired books along with prices. After receiving the money, purchase the books and give them to the persons who provided the funds so they can inscribe the books and get acquainted with them. There could be a special dedication service during which members of the congregation bring their gift books and present them to the church.

2. Let it be known through the usual communication channels in the church that Bible study resources are very appropriate memorial gifts.

3. Encourage women's, men's, couples', youth, and other groups in the church to accept responsibility for a special fund-raising project in order to collect enough money to purchase Bible study resources.

4. Designate money in the budget annually to purchase additional Bible study resources for the church library.

Five specific types of Bible study resources are illustrated on the following pages. In addition there are brief descriptions of several other types of resources. Representative recommended titles are included in the Helpful Books list at the end of the chapter.

Study Bibles

Study Bibles are designed to assist teachers, students, and all readers of the Bible in their study. There are many different editions of study Bibles, but all have a number of features in common.

1. There are general articles on subjects such as the history of the Bible, the authority of Scripture, the development of the canon, and so on.

2. For the Old and New Testaments, and for each book of the Bible, there are several pages of introduction dealing with authorship, date, major themes, and other critical questions.

3. At the bottom of each page are extended notes that provide definitions to key words, comments on critical issues, and explanations of difficult concepts. (See sample page from Westminister Study Edition of the Bible.)

4. Usually there are several maps, representing various historical periods of biblical history.

5. Often study Bibles will have chronology charts, brief concordances, glossaries, and lists of items such as kings, parables, and miracles.

All teachers and students will find a good study Bible a valuable tool for understanding what is being communicated by the writers of Holy Scripture.

when the day shall dawn upon[f] us from on high

79　　to give light to those who sit in darkness and in the shadow of death,
　　　to guide our feet into the way of peace."

80And the child grew and became strong in spirit, and he was in the wilderness till the day of his manifestation to Israel.

"TO YOU IS BORN . . . A SAVIOR"

2 In those days a decree went out from Caesar Augustus that all the world should be enrolled. 2 This was the first enrollment, when Qui·ri'ni·us was governor of Syria. 3And all went to be enrolled, each to his own city. 4And Joseph also went up from Galilee, from the city of Nazareth, to Judea, to the city of David, which is called Bethlehem, because he was of the house and lineage of David, 5 to be enrolled with Mary, his betrothed, who was with child. 6And while they were there, the time came for her to be delivered. 7And she gave birth to her first-born son and wrapped him in swaddling cloths, and laid him in a manger, because there was no place for them in the inn.

8 And in that region there were shepherds out in the field, keeping watch over their flock by night. 9And an angel of the Lord appeared to them, and the glory of the Lord shone around them, and they were filled with fear. 10And the angel said to them, "Be not afraid; for behold, I bring you good news of a great joy which will come to all the people; 11 for to you is born this day in the city of David a Savior, who is Christ the Lord. 12And this will be a sign for you: you will find a babe wrapped in swaddling cloths and lying in a manger." 13And suddenly there was with the angel a multitude of the heavenly host praising God and saying,

14　　"Glory to God in the highest,
　　　and on earth peace among men with whom he is pleased!"[g]

15 When the angels went away from them into heaven, the shepherds said to one another, "Let us go over to Bethlehem and see this thing that has happened, which the Lord has made known to us." 16And they went with haste, and found Mary and Joseph, and the babe lying in a manger. 17And when they saw it they made known the saying which had been told them concerning this child; 18 and all who heard it wondered at what the shepherds told them. 19 But Mary kept all these things, pondering them in her heart. 20And the shepherds returned, glorifying and praising God for all they had heard and seen, as it had been told them.

THE PRESENTATION OF JESUS

21 And at the end of eight days, when he was circumcised, he was called Jesus, the name given by the angel before he was conceived in the womb.

22 And when the time came for their purification according to the law of Moses, they brought him up to Jerusalem to present him to the Lord 23 (as it is written in the law of the Lord, "Every male that opens the womb shall be called holy to the Lord") 24 and to offer a sacrifice according to what is said in the law of the Lord, "a pair of turtledoves, or two young pigeons." 25 Now there was a man in Jerusalem, whose

f Or whereby the dayspring will visit. Other ancient authorities read since the dayspring has visited
g Other ancient authorities read peace, good will among men

---

lates the Messianic title "Branch" in Jer. 23:5; Zech. 3:8; 6:12). v. 80. Cf. ch. 2:40, 52; but John, unlike Jesus, was an ascetic (cf. in the wilderness).

vv. 1, 2. No such decree by Augustus (31 B.C. to A.D. 14) is known. Cyrenius Quirinius was governor of Syria and made a census in Palestine for taxing purposes in A.D. 6 (Acts 5:37). In Egypt a census was made every fourteen years; the earliest known was in A.D. 6; an earlier one, if made, would have been in 8 B.C. Possibly Quirinius made one in Palestine about 8–6 B.C. He was not then governor of Syria, but might have been in Syria for a special purpose. vv. 8–20. To humble men of Israel comes

word of the birth of the universal Savior (v. 11), who is Israel's Christ (Messiah) and all men's rightful Lord. v. 9. glory. The luminous manifestation of the divine Presence; in v. 14 it means "praise." v. 14. The Gloria in Excelsis. with whom he is pleased, to whom God in Christ's birth is showing favor. peace, between God and man; almost equivalent to salvation (cf. Isa. 52:7; 57:19).

vv. 21–39. The Jewish Law is fulfilled (v. 39). v. 21. eight days. Cf. Lev. 12:3. name. Cf. ch. 1:31. v. 22. Cf. Lev. 12:2, 4. v. 23. Cf. Ex. 13:2, 12. v. 24. Cf. Lev. 12:8. Joseph and Mary were poor. v. 25. Simeon was waiting for the consolation of Israel,

Bible Dictionaries

We usually think of using a dictionary to find definitions, correct spelling, and pronunciation of words. Bible dictionaries include much more than definitions. There are brief articles that provide much background information for key words. Depending upon the size of the volume, the articles could be as brief as a paragraph or as long as several pages. There are multivolume dictionaries with articles that are very comprehensive, one-volume dictionaries with articles that are more modest in length, and pocket-size Bible dictionaries in which the articles are very brief, seldom more than a paragraph or two. The sample article on "Bethlehem" is from *The New Westminster Dictionary of the Bible,* a one-volume dictionary with more than a thousand pages. Notice that the article includes correct spelling and pronunciation, the origin of the word, references to where the word is used in the Old and New Testaments, and some interpretive comments regarding the significance of Bethlehem.

Personally, after using a study Bible I find that the next most valuable resource is a Bible dictionary. Since background information about biblical passages and concepts is so limited in the curriculum, teachers will find such a book an invaluable aid in their preparation for teaching.

Beth′-le·hem (bĕth′lĕ-hĕm) [house of bread; rather, house of the god Laḥmu or of the goddess Laḥamu]. 1. A town in the hill country of Judah, originally called Ephrath; hence, to distinguish it from a place of the same name in Zebulun, called also Bethlehem-judah and Bethlehem Ephrathah (Gen. 35: 19; Judg. 17: 7, AV; Micah 5: 2). Bethlehem is not mentioned among the cities assigned to Judah (Josh., ch. 15; but given in v. 59, LXX). As a village it existed as early as the time of Jacob. Rachel died and was buried in its vicinity (Gen. 35: 16, 19; 48: 7). Its citizens were hospitable to the Levites (Judg. 17: 7; 19: 1). A branch of Caleb's family settled in the town and attained to great influence (I Chron. 2: 51, 54; cf. Ruth 4: 20). It was the residence of Boaz, of Ruth (Ruth 1: 19; 4: 9-11), doubtless of Obed (Ruth 4: 21-22), and of Jesse, the father of David (Ruth 4: 11, 17; I Sam. 16: 1, 4). As the birthplace and ancestral home of David, it was the city of David (Luke 2: 11). It was a walled town as early as the time of David. It fell temporarily into the hands of the Philistines (II Sam. 23: 14-15). Rehoboam strengthened its fortifications (II Chron. 11: 6). Bethlehemites returned from captivity with Zerubbabel (Ezra 2: 21; Neh. 7: 26).

It was looked to as the place where the Messiah should be born (Micah 5: 2; Matt. 2: 5), and accordingly when the fullness of time was come, Jesus became incarnate at Bethlehem. Jesus was born at Bethlehem because Joseph and Mary had to go there in order to be enrolled for taxation. The evidence suggests that this practice began in the time of Augustus (31 B.C.–A.D. 14). Another example of this form of taxation is found in an Egyptian papyrus, which says that in A.D. 103–104 there was a census in which people had to return to their ancestral homes for registration. In the vicinity of Bethlehem the annunciation to the shepherds took place (Luke 2: 1-20). To this place the Magi went to salute the newborn babe, and it was the infants of Bethlehem "and in all that region who were two years old or under," who were murdered by Herod to make sure that among them he had cut off the future king (Matt. 2: 1-18). There has never been any doubt as to its site. It is 5 miles s. of Jerusalem, at the modern village of Beit Laḥm, on the e. and n.e. slope of a long ridge, which to the w. is higher than the village. A little e. of the town is the church built by Helena, the mother of Constantine, over the cave said to be the stable in which the Nativity took place. Half a mile to the n. of the town is the traditional tomb of Rachel.

Bible Commentaries

The next most valuable resource is a Bible commentary. A commentary is exactly what the title implies; it is a book that provides comments on every verse or passage. There are multivolume commentaries with extensive comments and interpretations for each verse of each book of the Bible. Some multivolume sets are very technical and detailed, using a lot of Hebrew and Greek. There are other very fine multivolume commentaries written especially for lay readers and teachers in the church. The sample is from *The Layman's Bible Commentary*. One or two sets of different multivolume commentaries should be available in the church library. Teachers will find that a single-volume commentary will ordinarily be available and manageable for their use, but it will also be quite limited because the comments for each passage are so brief. A good study Bible and dictionary will ordinarily be as useful as a single-volume commentary.

Birth of Messiah (2:1-21)

The story of the birth of Jesus is the most amazing "good news" (vs. 10) ever to fall on human ears. Here is the hinge on which history turns, the dividing point between old and new, the single event which gives meaning to all other events. And yet, how naturally it is told. Two verses suffice to tell all that took place at the birth (vss. 6-7). Nothing unusual happened, save that the child was born in a stable, had a cattle trough for his first cradle, and his mother was probably unattended (vs. 7 implies that Mary herself wrapped him in swaddling cloths). "How silently the wondrous gift is given!" The birth of a baby, like millions of other babies, save poorer and more unnoticed than most—and God has entered human life! Would it have been told this way if it were not true?

The historical situation in which Luke sets the birth of Jesus has long been the subject for debate. Jesus lived in Nazareth, in Galilee. Why, then, was he born in Bethlehem of Judea? Some have seen Old Testament proof-texting at work here. Micah said something about Messiah's birth in Bethlehem (Micah 5:2). Therefore, it is alleged, Matthew and Luke contrived to have him born there to fulfill this prophecy. Of Luke this can hardly be said, for he makes no direct use of the Micah prophecy. Furthermore, the Jewish conceptions of the Messiah were varied, and in some of them Bethlehem played no role (John 7:27). Hence, it was not really necessary to have Jesus born in Bethlehem to believe in him as Messiah.

Former study failed to find an enrollment under Quirinius earlier than A.D. 7, although Jesus was born likely somewhere between 7 B.C. and 4 B.C. (see the discussion of 1:5-25). More recent study, however, has produced evidence tending to support Luke in his historic facts. It is known that the Romans forced owners of property to return to the place of the possession to have it recorded for tax purposes. These enrollments sometimes took years—40 years in Gaul!—for they were strongly resisted. It is quite possible that the enrollment under Quirinius was begun long before A.D. 7, and that Luke's historic facts are exact.

To be overly concerned about this, however, is to miss the point of Luke's reference. He was not at all interested in giving us the precise date of Jesus' birth. He was rather doing something much more profound. He was giving us the clue to the meaning of history. By the decree of Augustus the Messiah was born where God had chosen. In setting the Babe over against the Caesar, Luke is proclaiming that *God is Lord of history*. History is ruled not by fate, nor by the will of man, but by God. Not Caesar, but Christ, is Lord (vs. 11).

Jesus' birth is set over against the Caesar, too, because Jesus is "a Savior" (vs. 11). Augustus was called "savior." His word was called "gospel" (see the Introduction). But Augustus' "good news" would ultimately turn to bad news. His "salvation" could

Bible Concordances

A concordance is an alphabetical listing of the important words in a book, with references to the passages in which they occur. Without a concordance, persons are limited in their ability to find passages in the Bible by what they remember, by what they can find by leafing through, or by what they are directed to by other resources. A concordance is used for two purposes: to find passages for which one does not know the chapter and verse; and to find passages that include the same key word. There are two basic types of concordances.

1. Complete, comprehensive concordances include every word in the Bible. (Sample: *Analytical Concordance of the Bible*, Robert Young [Funk & Wagnalls, 1883])

2. Concise concordances are much smaller and include only the most familiar, most important, or most representative passages related to key words in the Bible.
(Sample: The *RSV Handy Concordance* [Zondervan Publishing House, 1972])

We have reprinted samples from both types of concordances, using the word *Bethlehem*. Usually the pastor and/or church library will have a complete concordance which could be borrowed by a teacher if one were needed. The concise concordance will usually be sufficient for most uses.

BETH LE'-HEM, בֵּית לֶחֶם *place of food.*
1. This town, about 6 miles south of Jerusalem, is celebrated as the birthplace of the Saviour. It was called Ephrath, and is mentioned as the place at which Rachel died and was buried, B.C. 1729. Rehoboam fortified or rebuilt it, B.C. 973. David was born here (circ. B.C. 1085), and hence it was called the city of David. Helena, the mother of Constantine, A.D. 325, erected a church, which remains to this day, on the place of the Nativity. It was ceded, with other towns, to Frederick II. by the sultan of Egypt in 1229. It was called Bethlehem-Judah to distinguish it from Bethlehem in Zebulon (Josh. 19. 15, 16). Bethlehem was made a bishopric in 1110.

Gen. 35. 19 buried in the way to Ephrath, which (is) B.
   48. 7 the way of Ephrath ; the same (is) B.
Judg 17. 7 there was a young man out of B.
   17. 8 And the man departed out of..B. to
   17. 9 he said..I (am) a Levite of B., and I go
   19. 1 a..Levite..took..a concubine out of B.
   19. 2 his concubine..went away from him..to B.
   19. 18 We (are) passing from B. toward..mount
   19. 18 I went to B., but I (am now) going to the
Ruth 1. 1 a certain man of B. went to sojourn in
   1 2 Mahlon and Chilion, Ephrathites of B.
   1. 19 they two went until they came to B.
   1. 19 when they were come to B...they said
   1. 22 they came to B. in the beginning of..har.
   2. 4 Boaz came from B., and said unto the
   4. 11 worthily in Ephratah..be famous in B.
1 Sa. 16. 4 Samuel..came to B...And the elders of
   17. 12 David..son of that Ephrathite of B.
   17. 15 David went..to feed his..sheep at B.
   20. 6 David..asked..that he might run to B.
   20. 28 David earnestly asked (leave..to go) to B.
2 Sa. 2. 32 buried him in the sepulchre..(in) B.
   23. 14 the garrison of the Philistines (was..in) B.
   23. 15 the water of the well of B...by the gate !
   23. 16 and drew water out of the well of B.
   23. 24 Elhanan the son of Dodo of B.
1 Ch. 11. 16 the Philistines' garrison (was) then at B.
   11. 17 the water of the well of B...at the gate
   11. 18 and drew water out of the well of B.
   11. 26 Elhanan the son of Dodo of B.
2 Ch. 11. 6 He built even B., and Etam, and Tekoa
Ezra 2. 21 children of B., an hundred twenty and
Neh. 7. 26 of B. and Netophah, an hundred fourscore
Jer. 41. 17 Chimham, which is by B., to go to..Egyp.
Mic. 5. 2 But thou, B... (though) thou be little
Matt. 2. 1 Jesus was born in B. of Judea, in the
   2. 5 they said unto him, In B. of Judea
   2. 6 And thou, B...art not the least among the
   2. 8 he sent them to B., and said, Go and
   2. 16 Then Herod..slew all the children..in B.
Luke 2. 4 Joseph..went..unto the city..called B.
   2. 15 the shepherds said..Let us now go..u. B.
John 7. 42 Christ cometh..out of the town of B.

BETHLEHEM
way to Ephrath (that is, *B*), Gen 35.19
on until they came to *B*. Ruth 1.19
commanded, and came to *B*. 1Sam 16.4
his father's sheep at *B*. 17.15
water out of the well of *B* 2Sam 23.16
But you, O *B* Ephrathah, who Mic 5.2
Now when Jesus was born in *B* of Mt 2.1
you, O *B*, in the land of Judah, 2.6
city of David,..called *B*, Lk 2.4
from David, and comes from *B*, Jn 7.42

Bible Atlases

We naturally think of maps when we think of an atlas, but Bible atlases usually contain more than a collection of maps. You will find chronology charts, geographical information, historical essays, and other background material related to the places, dates, events, and people that make up the biblical narrative. There are many portions of the Bible that are better understood when the reader has a sense of the geographic and historical setting in which they were written.

Other Bible Study Resources

We have identified the standard Bible study tools, but there are many other resources that could be used to guide teachers in their own study and preparation, as well as resources that could be used with the students.

Children's Bibles—There are many children's Bibles on the market, usually edited versions of the complete Bible, omitting large portions that are judged inappropriate for children. Many are attractively illustrated, which contributes to understanding a passage through a visual medium. Children's Bibles should never be used exclusively in lieu of a complete, standard translation, however, because children may get the impression that the Bible is just another children's book.

Bible Handbooks—Most major publishers of Bible study resources have in their catalogs a Bible handbook. These are valuable resources which contain numerous articles on a wide variety of biblical subjects. They will usually include charts, maps, chronologies, and lists, in addition to introductions or outlines for each book of the Bible.

Bible Introductions—There are many excellent books that provide introductory overviews of the whole Bible, or of the Old and New Testaments separately. Some are quite extensive, while others are very brief, providing more of a summary of basic information. Those that are illustrated with photographs, charts, and maps are not only visually attractive but make for interesting reading.

Bible Storybooks—Many good books present the narrative of the whole biblical story, or of particular stories. Usually written in an engaging, popular style and beautifully illustrated to help the biblical story come to life for the reader, these books are not just for children. However, teachers need to review these books carefully to be sure the textual and visual material provides responsible, appropriate interpretations of the biblical passages represented.

HELPFUL BOOKS

About Developing Bible Skills

Study Bibles

The Holy Bible, Westminster Study Edition. Revised Standard Version. Wm. Collins & Sons, 1965.

The New Oxford Annotated Bible. Revised Standard Version. Ed. Herbert G. May and Bruce M. Metzger. Oxford University Press, 1962.

The New English Bible with Apocrypha. Oxford Study Edition. Oxford University Press, 1976.

Harper Study Bible: The Holy Bible, Revised Standard Version. Harper & Row, 1962.

Bible Dictionaries

Harper's Bible Dictionary. Revised Edition. Madeleine S. Miller and J. Lane Miller. Harper & Row, 1974.

The New Westminster Dictionary of the Bible. Ed. Henry Snyder Gehman. Westminster Press, 1969.

The Westminster Concise Bible Dictionary. Barbara Smith. Westminster Press, 1981.

Single-Volume Bible Commentaries

The Interpreter's One-Volume Commentary on the Bible. Ed. Charles M. Laymon. Abingdon Press, 1971.

The Abingdon Bible Commentary. Ed. Frederick Carl Eiselen, Edwin Lewis, and David G. Downey. Abingdon Press, 1929; Doubleday, 1979.

The New Layman's Bible: Commentary in One Volume. Ed. G. C. D. Howley et al. Zondervan.

Multivolume Bible Commentaries

The Daily Study Bible. Revised Edition. 27 vols. (More being developed.) New Testament, ed. William Barclay; Old Testament, ed. John C. L. Gibson. Westminster Press.

The Layman's Bible Commentary. 25 vols. John Knox Press, 1964.

The Interpreter's Bible. 12 vols. Ed. George A. Buttrick. Abingdon Press, 1952–57.

The Interpreter's Concise Commentary. 8 vols. (Previously published as The Interpreter's One-Volume Commentary on the Bible.) Abingdon Press, 1983.

Bible Concordances

The RSV Handy Concordance. Zondervan, 1962.

Harper's Topical Concordance. Ed. Charles R. Jay. Harper & Row, 1976.

Strong's Exhaustive Concordance of the Bible. Ed. James Strong (d. 1894). Abingdon Press.

Nelson's Complete Concordance to the Revised Standard Version Bible. Ed. John William Ellison. Thomas Nelson, 1978.

Bible Atlases

Oxford Bible Atlas. 2nd Edition. Ed. Herbert G. May and G. H. Hunt. Oxford University Press, 1974.

The Westminster Historical Atlas to the Bible. Revised Edition. G. Ernest Wright and Floyd V. Filson. Westminster Press, 1956.

Discovering the Biblical World. Harry Thomas Frank. Harper & Row, 1975.

Bible Handbooks

Abingdon Bible Handbook. Ed. Edward P. Blair. Abingdon Press, 1975.

Eerdmans' Concise Bible Handbook. David Alexander and Patricia Alexander. Eerdmans Publishing Co., 1981.

Eerdmans' Concise Bible Encyclopedia. Ed. Patricia Alexander. Eerdmans Publishing Co., 1981.

Harper's Encyclopedia of Bible Life. Revised Edition. Madeline S. Miller and J. Lane Miller. Harper & Row, 1983.

Bible Introductions

Understanding the Old Testament. Third Edition. Ed. Bernhard W. Anderson. Prentice Hall, 1975.
Understanding the New Testament. Fourth Edition. Howard Clark Kee and Franklin W. Young. Prentice Hall, 1983.
How to Read the New Testament. Etienne Charpentier. Crossroads Press, 1982.
How to Read the Old Testament. Etienne Charpentier. Crossroads Press, 1982.
Harper's Introduction to the Bible. Gerald Hughes and Stephen Travis. Harper & Row, 1981.
Harper's World of the New Testament. Edwin M. Yamauchi, Harper & Row, 1981.

Children's Bibles

International Children's Version, New Testament. Sweet Publishing Co., 1983.
Taize Picture Bible. (Based on the Jerusalem Bible.) Fortress Press, 1969.
Young Readers Bible. Abingdon Press, 1965.

Teaching the Bible

Furnish, Dorothy Jean. *Exploring the Bible with Children.* Abingdon Press, 1975.
Furnish, Dorothy Jean. *Living the Bible with Children.* Abingdon Press, 1979.
Griggs, Donald L. *20 New Ways of Teaching the Bible.* Abingdon Press, 1977.
Griggs, Patricia. *Using Storytelling in Christian Education.* Abingdon Press, 1981.
Mass, Robin. *Church Bible Study Handbook.* Abingdon Press, 1982.
March, W. Eugene. *Basic Bible Study: Revised Edition.* Geneva Press, 1984.
Weber, Hans-Ruedi. *Experiments with Bible Study.* Westminster Press, 1981.
Wink, Walter. *Transforming Bible Study.* Abingdon Press, 1980.

CHECKLIST FOR TEACHERS

1. Have I mastered the skill of quickly finding the Bible passages I am looking for?
   _____completely   _____mostly   _____barely

2. To what extent are the Bible skills I use with the students appropriate to *their* abilities?

   _____students are seldom successful
   _____students are successful when helped
   _____students are usually successful on their own

3. What kinds of activities have I been using to be sure my students know how to find Bible passages?

   _____
   _____
   _____
   _____
   _____

4. What strategies have I been using to help my students read passages with understanding?

   _____
   _____
   _____
   _____

5. How often do I use Bible footnotes and cross-reference notes when I am preparing for teaching?
   _____always   _____often   _____seldom   _____never

6. Which Bible study resources are available to me in the church library or in my own library, and which ones do I use?

Available		Use
_____	Bible dictionary	_____
_____	single-volume Bible commentary	_____
_____	multivolume Bible commentary	_____
_____	Bible concordance	_____
_____	Bible handbook	_____
_____	Bible introductions	_____

7. Which of the above resources have I used with my students?

   _____
   _____
   _____

8. Which of the above resources would I like to use with them?

_____

_____

_____

_____

9. Which of the above resources need to be purchased and available in multicopies in the church library?

_____

_____

_____

_____

10. If I were to buy one or two Bible study tools for myself, which one(s) would I buy?

_____

_____

_____

SUGGESTIONS FOR EDUCATION LEADERS

1. Place on the agenda of an education committee meeting this question: "How can we make available to teachers and students the essential Bible study tools and encourage them to use the tools in their studying, planning, and teaching?" There should be some preparation before discussing this question:

Take an inventory of the church library to see what Bible study tools are available.

Review the curriculum to determine which Bible study tools are needed and/or recommended.

Poll the teachers to see what Bible study tools they have personally, which ones they feel they need, and which ones they might use if they had them.

Review the church budget to see how much money would be available to purchase new resources.

Consider other strategies for securing funds to purchase Bible study tools for teachers and students.

2. We should not assume that all teachers know the basics—abbreviations of Bible books, how to use footnotes and cross references, and what Bible dictionaries, commentaries, concordances, and atlases are and how to use them. A workshop on basic Bible skills should be offered regularly for teachers, as well as for other adults and the youth of the congregation. A strategy should be designed that provides ample opportunities for all participants to work on one skill or with one resource at a time and practice with it long enough to feel comfortable and confident. I have been impressed again and again with the appreciation of people when they are introduced to these basic skills and tools. After about an hour of working with concordances, almost every person in one group wanted to buy the concordance he or she was using. Not one person there had a personal concordance. Since the group was so highly motivated, I decided to sell those people the concordances and use the proceeds to replace them. One person said to me afterward, "I always knew there was an easier way to find passages in the Bible. Now I won't ever feel helpless again."

3. A church might consider making Bible study tools available to all the members, especially teachers. Upgrade the church library and, through promotion and encouragement, help the members realize the value of using the Bible study tools that are in the church library. It is possible to establish a Book Nook where quantities of basic books are available for purchase. Often churches can arrange for a discount when books are ordered in quantity. Bible study resources are quite expensive, so any discount that can be passed on to the members will be much appreciated. I personally think it would be worth the investment to give teachers a book for each year they teach. I would encourage them to buy their own personal study Bible, and then give them . . .
    . . . a Bible dictionary the first year.
    . . . a concise Bible concordance the second year.
    . . . a small Bible atlas the third year.
    . . . a Bible handbook the fourth year.

4. A church educator, superintendent, or committee would find it very worthwhile to review the curriculum for the children's and youths' classes, to see whether there are units that emphasize the developing of Bible skills, and which Bible study tools are included. If such skills and tools are not featured at some point in each year's curriculum, arrangements should be made to supplement the curriculum to include these important activities.

Chapter Five

ENABLING CREATIVITY

Usually when I speak with teachers about the subject of creativity, at least one of them will say, "I am not very creative." I think these people mean that they are not very artistic, as compared to skillful painters, musicians, sculptors, writers, and other such people. It may be very true that they lack the skills of an artist, but it is not true that they are thereby uncreative. Creativity is not limited to inventors, artists, and musicians; to be imaginative, curious, innovative, or expressive in any realm of one's life is to be creative. Creativity has been defined as "any thinking or planning process which solves a problem in an original and useful way." According to that definition I would say that teachers in the church are very creative—they solve a multitude of problems every time they plan and teach a lesson.

Creativity is a gift from God given to all people. God is the One we know as Creator—Creator of the universe and of our world. We worship the Creator when we experience the gifts of God in the majesty of a sunset, the beauty of a flowering rose, the miracle of the birth of a child. God not only has created a world, God has created us in the image of our Creator. Part of what it means to be created in the image of God is that we have the potential for participating as partners with God in the continual process of creating and re-creating. One of the gifts we each receive at birth is the ability to think, to feel, and to express ourself in unique and creative ways. An aspect of our ministry as teachers is to offer our creative selves to God so that our gifts may be used for the benefit of those we teach. Another aspect of our ministry is to relate to students in such a way as to enable them to see themselves as persons created in God's own image, endowed with their own special gifts of creativity. To say, "I'm not creative," is, in a sense, to deny an aspect of our humanity as unique, special individuals, created in the image of God.

In Chapter 2, I emphasized the importance of encouraging students to participate actively in their learning. To plan activities that invite students to become actively involved in the learning process requires a lot of creativity on the part of the teacher. Also, to participate purposefully and enthusiastically calls forth a lot of creativity from the student. A key to motivating students to participate is that they be encouraged to express themselves in creative ways. In Chapter 3 I suggested that when planning a session, it is important to include that part of the lesson in which students are invited to respond creatively to what they are studying. After the students have been introduced to a subject, have gained some background information, and have had a chance to explore the subject to some extent, they are well equipped to respond—to express in some creative way what they personally think, feel, or believe. Sufficient time should be planned for this part of the session because creative expression cannot be hurried. When students have had the opportunity to express themselves, teachers will have considerable evidence to indicate whether objectives have been accomplished.

With Chapters 2 and 3 as a foundation, in this chapter I would like to explore the subject of creativity in more depth. We will discuss the nature of creativity, describe factors that hinder and others that encourage creativity, present a process that produces creativity, and outline some examples of creative writing.

The Nature of Creativity

The source of all creativity is the One who is Creator of all there is. According to the biblical witness, God creates and re-creates continually in the entire natural order, and in human life. All humanity is created in the image of God—not to look like God as a reflected image, but to be like God as an imprinted image. Each teacher and student is created in that image; each is endowed with the gifts of remembering, searching, thinking, loving, and expressing. These gifts enable them to reach within themselves and beyond themselves to share their lives with one another. In whatever way this sharing occurs, when it is genuine, personal, and meaningful, it is truly the result of having participated in the process of creating and re-creating. Present within all persons is the potential for hearing and responding to God's Word in ways that are special and uniquely appropriate to their own life situations. Teachers are creative when they . . .

> . . . use their own skills, ideas, and experiences to help them communicate with those they teach.
>
> . . . relate to their students in personal, sensitive, and helpful ways.
>
> . . . adapt the given curriculum resources to the particular needs, interests, and abilities of their students.
>
> . . . seek to relate the subject they are teaching to the life and faith experiences of their students.
>
> . . . show flexibility in departing from their lesson plan to respond to immediate concerns of the students.
>
> . . . improvise when the expected time, resources, or materials are not available.
>
> . . . ask or answer questions prompted by the immediate situation, rather than by what is in the manual.

Teachers not only are creative within themselves, but they can contribute significantly to enabling the students to become more creative. Teachers help students to be creative when they . . .

> . . . establish an atmosphere of trust, caring, and acceptance.
>
> . . . provide opportunities for students to make choices as to how they will express themselves.
>
> . . . offer a variety of materials, methods, or resources from which students can choose.
>
> . . . demonstrate their openness to many different responses and expressions.

. . . accept and reinforce what the students say and do in their own creative expressions.

. . . invite students to draw upon their own experiences in order to express what they think, feel, and believe.

Creativity is the result of a number of factors. The rich experiences provided by living with people, reading, traveling, being exposed to a variety of media, stimulating study or work—all provide the raw material with which to be creative. However, the experiences themselves are not enough. It is the reflection on the experiences—trying to understand them and relate them to a larger perspective—that is necessary to generate creativity.

The ability to trust oneself, as well as others, is another important factor. If we are unsure of ourselves, cautious, afraid we will say or do something wrong, then it is very difficult for us to take the risk necessary to probe the unknown and to be creative. When we believe with certainty that we are already accepted and loved by God, no matter what we say or do, then we can have some confidence in ourselves to try to express what we think. When we are open to new ideas and experiences, when we appreciate and value new ways of perceiving reality, when we are free of any threat of physical or psychological harm, we are then in a postition to express ourselves creatively. These and a number of other factors either hinder or facilitate creativity.

Factors That Hinder Creativity

Too Much Concern About Being Correct—If the teacher implies that there is a predetermined way to carry out an activity and that all the students should end up with exactly the same results, the students will be more concerned about doing it correctly than about expressing themselves freely.

Too Much Dependence upon the Teacher—Some students want to please the teacher in everything they do. They keep checking with the teacher to see if they are doing it right, continually seeking teacher's approval. If teachers allow the students to continue to be strongly dependent upon them, rather than encouraging them to be more independent, they will hinder the student's creativity.

Unrealistic Expectations—There are times when students think that their work must have the quality of a work of art. At other times, teachers expect students to express themselves with words, concepts, or images that are beyond their grasp or ability. When expectations are unrealistic, students often will give up before they even try to be creative.

Mistakes Are Unacceptable—Part of being creative is trying new ways, exploring, experimenting with ideas and images, materials and processes. Much learning happens during this trial-and-error approach. If students get the idea that mistakes are unacceptable, they will not put forth much energy to be creative.

Little Room for Self-expression—When all that is required is to connect the dots, color the illustrations, cut along the lines, fill in the blanks, or find the correct words, not much creativity is being called forth. A printed workbook, packaged activity, or prescribed process hinders creativity. A blank piece of paper with a pencil or a few colored markers would greatly enhance creativity.

Factors That Encourage Creativity

Each of the above items can be turned around, approached from a different direction, and seen as a positive factor. In addition, there are a number of other factors that can encourage the creativity of students.

An Open, Interesting, Inviting Environment—The room arrangement, the atmosphere of the space, the attitudes of the teachers, and the availability of a variety of resources—all contribute to an environment that says, "Welcome, we are glad you are here. Please feel free to express yourself."

A Focus on Problem Solving Rather Than on Answer Giving—When students sense a problem, dilemma, or issue that requires their own insights and skills, they are much more likely to be motivated to respond creatively than if they think the teacher already has the solution and is just testing them.

Opportunities to Make Choices—When seeking to interpret a passage of Scripture, students will be much more creative if they have the options of speaking, writing, illustrating, or acting out their interpretations, rather than being limited to just one mode.

Time to Experiment or Warm Up—Seldom does anyone feel satisfied with the "first draft" of anything. It is important to have time to redo, restate, or try another way to produce something that will be worthwhile. Having one sheet of paper for practice and another for the finished product will help students become more creative.

Need for Acceptance and Respect—The emotional environment is as important as the physical environment for encouraging creativity. In verbal and nonverbal ways, teachers can communicate that at this time and place, students will be listened to, accepted, encouraged, trusted, and respected.

A Process to Enable Creativity

Even though creativity is characterized by spontaneity, openness, and individual expression, there is a specific process which teachers can follow to facilitate that creativity among the students. The steps of the process follow in a necessary logical order, and all the steps must be taken in order to have some assurance that students will express themselves.

In order to understand the process, let's imagine a situation of two teachers and twelve to fifteen students in the middle of a study unit focused on the friends and followers of Jesus. The unit includes a series of passages from the Gospels, showing what happened to particular persons—Nicodemus, Andrew, Mary Magdalene, Zacchaeus, Matthew, Mary (Martha's sister), and Thomas—as a result of their encounters with Jesus.

The *opening* of the session invites the students to recall important persons in their own lives. They should think about persons who have made a difference in the way they think, feel, or believe. In pairs or in small groups each of the students talks about one person and how that person influenced his or her life.

In the *presenting* part of the session, the teacher introduces information about the many people who encountered Jesus and how their lives were changed. To illustrate the point, the

teacher may want to tell the story of the blind man, Bartimaeus, whose sight was restored when he met Jesus.

During the *exploring* time, students are asked to select one of the several persons named above to be the focus of further study. After each has chosen one person to explore, they work in pairs or in small groups with others who have chosen the same person. They are given one or more Bible passages to read, and they have available some Bible study resource books. Their exploration is directed by three questions: (1) Why did the person and Jesus meet? (2) What happened to the person because of his or her encounter with Jesus? and (3) What feelings do you think the person had toward Jesus? Time is allowed to compare notes and share answers. To *respond creatively*, the students are given several options:

1. Write a short article for the *Jerusalem Journal*, presenting interesting and important information about the person.

2. Prepare a dialogue of an interview between the person who met Jesus and another imaginary person.

3. Work with Write-On slides to develop a set of slides to illustrate the story of the encounter between the person and Jesus.

During the *closing*, the students have an opportunity to share with one another what they have created to express their understanding of a person's encounter with Jesus.

With this sample lesson plan as a frame of reference, consider these steps, which should enable the students to be successful in their creative expression.

Step One: Set the stage.

In the *opening* activity the students are drawn into the session by eliciting from their own experiences something that is related to what will come later in the session. They are able to speak freely from their own experience without having to worry about whether their responses are correct.

Step Two: Provide information.

Through the *presenting* and *exploring* activities, the students are gaining information about the persons who encountered Jesus. The information is provided by the teacher, the Bible, the resource books, and the other students. The gathering of the information is directed by three questions. Though these two parts of the session are tightly structured, the students do have an opportunity to make several important choices and to work in a self-directed manner.

Step Three: Offer several options.

There are three possible ways the students can *respond* to the information they have gained. In our sample lesson each of the three options represents a different medium, so that whether the students have abilities in writing, speaking, or illustrating, there should be one activity that interests each person. Students will be much more creative when they have chosen their media and are free to express themselves in any way in those media.

Step Four: Arrange for necessary materials.

All creative activities will require some materials. These should be gathered ahead of time and be immediately available so that no time is wasted getting started with the activity.

Step Five: Give easy-to-follow directions.

There should be a written outline of directions for each of the three optional activities, so that the students can work at their own pace and know exactly what they need to do in order to be successful with the activities.

Step Six: Allow sufficient time.

Students should not be rushed as they work on their activities. Teachers should indicate ahead of time how much time is available and give a reminder midway through the activity. Activities that will take a lot of time can be spread over two or more sessions.

71

Step Seven: Be available and supportive.

Teachers should neither hover over the students nor remove themselves completely. They should be present and available, and remain alert to whether any students need help. By circulating among them, spending brief moments in conversation, and being sensitive to their needs, teachers can be very supportive of the students in their creative efforts.

Step Eight: Provide opportunities for sharing.

Students should be invited to share the results of their creativity. The sharing will be most effective if it is not required or forced, and it is best to include it as a natural part of the session plan, not just as a show-and-tell exercise. Teachers should not function as judges of an "art show" but rather as friends who appreciate the efforts of all the students. If the creative work is to be displayed for others, *all* the work should be displayed, not just a few that are judged best.

Some Possibilities for Enabling Creativity

There are hundreds of possible activities and resources that can enable the creativity of students. In the teacher's manual of the curriculum, there are suggested learning activities for each session. Some are so structured that there is little possibility for the students to express themselves creatively. Often the activities found in students' books are quite limiting, especially when they call for filling in the blanks, connecting the dots, cutting and pasting and coloring. These are examples of activities that serve to reinforce the remembering of important information. Reinforcement activities are often helpful and necessary, but they are not creative. Teachers should not presume that because students enjoy such reinforcement activities that they are at the same time expressing themselves creatively. The above lesson plan illustrated a way to involve the students in a process that would encourage them to connect in a more personal way with people whose lives had been influenced by Jesus. Starting with a blank sheet of paper to write an imaginary article for the *Jerusalem Journal* moves beyond just remembering information toward personal creative expression. Drawing on a dozen blank Write-On slides is much more creative than cutting, pasting, and coloring someone else's illustrations. Both activities have a place in the session plan—one for reinforcing important information, the other for eliciting the student's own interpretative expression.

It is not possible in this short chapter to describe the very many examples of creative activities appropriate for various age groups. The bibliography for this chapter lists a number of books, each of which is full of specific directions for a wide variety of activities. The next chapter also provides many suggestions for creative ways teachers and students can use audio visuals. To conclude this chapter I would like to describe eight different creative writing activities. Writing is something that can be done by children as young as nine or ten, as well as by adults. The description for each activity is accompanied by sample directions to guide the students. The eight writing activities are presented in order from least to most personal involvement.

Acrostic Poems

Acrostic is an ancient form of structured verse, used even by the psalmists in the Old Testament. The poem is formed by using the name of a person, place, title, topic, or other subject. The word is written vertically so that each letter is the first letter of another word or phrase. Most acrostics are written in free verse, but it is possible to create rhyme and meter as well.

Directions

1. Read Acts, chapter 2.
2. Select a key word to form an acrostic.
3. Write a word or phrase beginning with each letter of the key word.
4. After finishing one acrostic, try two or three more, focusing on Acts 2.
5. Share what you have written.

Sample

S   pirit of God comes with
P   ower in the
I   ncarnation and
R   esurrection of Jesus the Christ
I   n our lives
T   oday

Cinquain Poems

Cinquain (sin-can) is a poetry form that originated in France. The first line contains the title (a noun, one word); the second line describes the title (two words); the third line contains action words or phrase (three words); the fourth line contains feeling words related to the title (four words); the fifth line is the conclusion, or punchline (one word).

Directions

1. Focus on the Apostle Paul, using a Bible dictionary or the book *People of the Bible* to gain information about Paul in relation to the early church.
2. Create a cinquain poem starting with the title "Paul" and another with the title "Church."
3. Share what you have written.

Sample

Paul
Traveling   Missionary
Proclaiming   the   Gospel
With   love,   power,   conviction
Apostle

Crossword Puzzle

A crossword puzzle can provide a challenging reinforcement activity to help students learn and remember facts. The creation of a crossword puzzle has even greater potential as students select words and create definitions of words for clues focused on a particular subject. It is not necessary to create symmetrical, complicated puzzles. For our purposes it is more helpful to select as many relevant words as possible and then create a puzzle in whatever form develops.

Directions

1. Decide on a key subject for the focus of the puzzle (Apostles, Paul, Church, Jerusalem, etc.).
2. Make a list of ten to twenty related words.
3. Start with one word, perhaps the longest, in a horizontal or vertical position in the center of a sheet of graph paper.
4. Be sure to use a pencil, so you can try words in various spaces and be able to erase them.
5. Use a clean sheet of paper to trace or outline the spaces to be occupied by the words. Number each word.
6. Make up a set of clues related to the words of the puzzle.
7. Make copies of the puzzle to share with others.

A Job Opening or Description

Employers prepare announcements of job openings to be published in newspapers and trade or professional journals. The announcements usually list qualifications, responsibilities, benefits, and so on. When persons are hired, they are often given a job description which lists duties and responsibilities.

Directions

1. Read Acts 1:12-26 and/or Acts 6:1-7.
2. Consider the qualifications and responsibilities of apostles and/or deacons.
3. Write an announcement of a "job" opening for an apostle or a deacon, or write a job description for the same position.
4. Share what you have written.

A Postcard or Letter

Persons often send postcards to family and friends when they travel. They also send letters to friends, to people in positions of responsibility, or to those in need. (Provide paper to simulate postcards and stationery.)

Directions

1. Read Acts 8:26-40.
2. Identify with either Philip or the Ethiopian official.

74

3. As if you were one or the other, write a postcard or letter to someone in your family or to a friend.
4. Share what you have written.

News Report

Reporters for radio, television, and newspapers write reports that describe events they or others have observed. Reporters try to answer these six questions: What? When? Where? Who? How? Why? Most reporters write in such a way that this essential information is included in the first paragraph or two. The remainder of the report expands upon the basic information.

Directions

1. Read one of the following passages describing an event in the life of Paul:

> Acts   16:16-40—in prison in Philippi
> 17:16-30—in Athens
> 19:21-41—riot in Ephesus
> 21:27-36—arrested in the Temple

2. Imagine yourself present as an observer of the event. Write out some questions to answer in writing a news report.
3. Write your news report.
4. Share with others by including in a class "newspaper."

Written Prayers

Prayers could be written from the perspective of a person's experience in the book of Acts. Or, prayers could be written that might be included as part of a worship service. In one sense, prayers are like letters—letters written to God.

Directions

1. Select a person or an event from the book of Acts with which to identify. Or, search for prayers that are included in Acts.
2. Read enough of the biblical text so that you have a frame of reference for writing a prayer.
3. Write a prayer as if you were a person present at one of the events in Acts. Or, write a paraphrase of one of the prayers in Acts.
4. Be ready to share your prayer during the closing session.

Statement of Belief

Persons and religious organizations often write out their basic beliefs in the form of a credo. One of the objectives of the preaching of Peter and Paul was to motivate people to respond with expressions of their own beliefs. Statements of belief can be as brief as a few key sentences or as long as several pages.

Directions

1. Read one of the following speeches or sermons in the book of Acts:

> Acts   2:14-39—Peter's sermon at Pentecost
> 7: 1-53—Stephen's speech
> 17:16-34—Paul in Athens
> 26: 1-23—Paul before King Agrippa

2. Read the speech or sermon as if it were spoken directly to you.
3. Respond with your own personal series of statements, beginning, "I believe . . . ."

HELPFUL BOOKS

About Enabling Creativity

Dotts, M. Franklin, and Dotts, Maryann J. *Clues to Creativity.* 3 vols. Friendship Press, 1974.

Durka, Gloria, and Smith, Joanmarie, editors. *Aesthetic Dimensions of Religious Education.* Paulist Press, 1979.

Griggs, Patricia. *Creative Activities in Church Education.* Abingdon Press, 1974.

LeFever, Marlene D. *Growing Creative Children.* Tyndale House Publishers, 1981.

Schaupp, Jack. *Creating and Playing Games with Students.* Abingdon Press, 1981.

Smith, Judy Gattis. *20 Ways to Use Drama in Teaching the Bible.* Abingdon Press, 1975.

Wankelman, Willard F.; Wigg, Philip; and Wigg, Marietta. *A Handbook of Arts and Crafts.* William C. Brown Co., 1974.

Wright, Kathryn S. *Let the Children Paint.* Seabury Press, 1966.

CHECKLIST FOR TEACHERS

1. What does it mean to me to be created in the image of God?

   _____
   _____
   _____

2. How often do I think or say, "I'm not creative"?
   ____never   ____seldom   ____frequently

3. If creativity is "solving problems in an original and useful way," what are some ways I have been creative recently?

   _____
   _____

4. When I look at the factors that hinder or encourage creativity, how am I doing in relation to my class?

   _____
   _____
   _____

5. Which types of activities do I plan most often?
   ____reinforcement activities   ____craft activities   ____creative activities

6. When students express themselves creatively, how do I usually respond?
   ____accepting and affirming   ____critically and judgmentally   ____indifferently

7. Do I offer a variety of creative activities during a unit of study, so that persons with different abilities and interests can find a meaningful way to express themselves?
   ____verbal activities   ____dramatic activities
   ____visual activities   ____musical activities

8. Do I allow sufficient time for creative activities in every lesson?
   ____always   ____most of the time   ____occasionally

SUGGESTIONS FOR EDUCATION LEADERS

1. Plan for a time to discuss with leaders and teachers the differences between reinforcement activities, craft activities, and creative activities.

Reinforcement activities focus on information and involve students in demonstrating that they know the information. Crossword puzzles, fill-in-the-blanks, find the words, and match sets of information—all are examples of reinforcing activities. These are very useful activities, but they are not creative activities.

Craft activities usually involve materials, patterns or recipes, specific procedures, and previously determined finished products. When two or more students are working on the same craft, they will have identical or quite similar end products. These also are very useful activities, but they are not creative activities.

Creative activities do not presume right answers or similar finished products. Students start with blank sheets of paper, formless hunks of clay, or unstructured periods of time and use the resources to express, in their own original way, something they want to share.

Teachers can be encouraged to review four to six previous lesson plans, to see the types of activities they use most often. They can also look at their lesson plans for the next week or two in order to plan for creative activities.

2. Often teachers will be more comfortable in planning and utilizing creative activities if they have had personal experience with them. In a workshop or in a portion of a teachers' meeting, they can be guided in working with one or two types of activities. Several or all the examples of creative writing activities can be introduced and time provided to practice one or more of the activities with which they are least familiar.

3. Teachers can discuss the two lists of factors that hinder and encourage creativity. They can then work in small groups (2 to 4 persons) to develop descriptions of one factor from each list. The descriptions developed by the small group can then be shared in the larger group.

4. Brainstorming is a very simple creative activity. The process involves focusing on a topic, task, problem, question, or issue. A period of time is designated for suggesting as many ideas or solutions as possible. Whatever comes to one's mind is offered. There are no judgments about whether the suggestions are worthwhile—every idea, even the wildest, is accepted and written down. After all ideas have been exhausted, the suggestions are evaluated, and those that will be most useful are selected.

Teachers can be invited to participate in brainstorming. The focus can be simple—"What are the best ways to use teaching pictures?" or more complex—"What can we do to improve attendance at church school?" After brainstorming, evaluating the suggestions, and deciding which to implement, there should be time for reflection. During that period, teachers can be invited to identify ways they have been creative and how they might implement a similar process with their students.

Chapter Six

USING
AUDIO VISUALS

Teachers in the church are caught in a dilemma. On the one hand, we live in an electronic age when it is possible to have instantaneous and simultaneous involvement with events and persons around the world. We have immediate access to more information about more subjects than any other generation in history. Through the utilization of satellites; computers; video cameras, recorders, and monitors; and all the other available audio-visual hardware and software, there is a great potential for increased communication and learning.

On the other hand, we are participants and believers in the good news of God's mighty acts of creation and redemption, summarized in a faith-story that had its origin in another part of the world more than thirty centuries ago. That faith-story has been communicated from generation to generation, primarily by persons who shared it with others through preaching, teaching, and personal witness.

Thus our dilemma: How do we reconcile the modern sophisticated, technological world in which we live with the ancient, simple, personal faith-story that gives meaning and direction to our lives? In our attempts to resolve that dilemma, we make several mistakes. We hop on the bandwagon to purchase all the equipment and resources we can afford in order to be as contemporary and relevant as possible. The problem is that we may become so fascinated with the technology that we forget the essence of the ministry to which we are called. Our ministry is helping, sharing, healing, and loving so that people may know the good news of Jesus Christ as their Savior.

Another mistake is to ignore the technological advances that increase our ability to communicate with others. We don't have much money to support the work of Christian education, so we cannot afford to purchase the latest equipment. Most of us feel we are not very competent in the operation of computers, video recorders, or even a filmstrip projector, so why go to all the effort and expense? The problem is that we may miss significant opportunities to communicate with persons who are very much influenced by the electronic environment in which they live.

We are mistaken if we think that any electronic medium can substitute for the human encounter between teacher and student. We are equally mistaken if we presume that the only way to teach is to depend solely upon the personal interaction between the teacher and the students.

To solve this dilemma, church teachers should develop communication skills that enable them to share the essence of the gospel personally. They also need to develop basic skills in utilizing various audio-visual resources to assist them in their teaching. Teachers should never be made to feel they must choose between relating to the students in personal ways and using audio visuals to present important information, but should be helped to see the value of both approaches.

There are several terms that need to be identified and explained—*media, audio visuals, hardware, and software*—before we proceed with the heart of this chapter.

Media is the plural of *medium*, which has several meanings. A medium is in the middle, between two other entities; it is a means by which information is transmitted from one party to another. Newspapers, radio, and television are spoken of as *mass media*, in that they transmit information about persons, events, and ideas from the source to the reader, listener, or viewer. In education we use the terms *multi media* and *media resources* to represent all the printed, projected, and recorded devices available for communicating subject matter. Media can be as sophisticated as a personal computer and a video recorder, or as basic and simple as a photograph and a filmstrip.

Audio visuals use sound and/or images to communicate information. Often the terms *audio visuals* and *media* are used interchangeably. For purposes of clarity and consistency, I will use *audio visuals* in this chapter because I think it is a term easily understood and most often used by church teachers.

Hardware refers to audio-visual equipment (the hard, heavy stuff) such as projectors, recorders, screens, speakers, cameras, and computers.

Software is the term used for materials or resources (the soft, flexible stuff) such as slides, films, tapes, photographs, filmstrips, and programs. When dealing with audio visuals it is essential to deal with both the equipment *and* the resources.

In this chapter we will focus on a number of general principles that are basic to understanding the importance of audio visuals, and we will consider several criteria for selecting and using audio visuals. The major section of the chapter outlines several ways to use each of five different types of audio visuals.

The Importance of Audio Visuals

Not only are audio visuals an accepted part of both religious and general education, but they are also very much a part of the daily life of most individuals of all ages. Children as young as kindergarten age are receiving simple computers as Christmas gifts. Video cassette recorders are found in millions of American homes. Young people are seen everywhere with lightweight earphones connected to miniature radios or recorders in their pockets. Cameras of many shapes and sizes are as common as wristwatches. And there is hardly a person in our country who isn't an expert at operating a television set. These examples illustrate the all-pervasive presence of audio-visual equipment and resources in the lives of children, youths, and adults in the classes, groups, and organizations of the church. This suggests to me that it is not a question of whether or not to use audio visuals, but rather of when to use which ones.

Audio visuals are more than an aid to the teacher seeking to communicate important information and ideas to students; they are most effective when used directly by the students. Students can use audio visuals in learning centers, as a way to explore a subject alone or with a small group, or as a means for expressing themselves creatively. It is one thing for the teacher to present a filmstrip about Moses to a student who sits, listens, and views passively. It is quite another to provide the motivation, the materials, and the time for a student to draw images for fifteen Write-On slides and write a script to accompany the slides, in order to summarize and interpret the story of Moses' call to return to Egypt. It is helpful to have available, and to use, commercially produced audio visuals; when they are well done, they can communicate effectively and efficiently the subject a teacher wants to share with the class. However, do-it-yourself audio visuals, produced by students and teachers from available materials may have a far greater impact on learning.

Some people are more verbally oriented; they assimilate and communicate information and ideas through the use of words more than by any other means. These people will find that books, lectures, stories, tape recordings, and phonograph records make a valuable contribution to their learning. Other people are more visually oriented; they are more adept at receiving and expressing information and ideas through visual images. These people will find films, photographs, charts, slides, filmstrips, and transparencies significant resources to facilitate their learning. When audio and visual resources are combined, as in a film, the learning capacity of every student is enhanced. Conversation and other forms of verbal interaction are very important in the teaching-learning process, but their value will be increased significantly when they are accompanied by a variety of audio visuals. A student who has difficulty reading about the prophet Jeremiah may be helped by viewing a filmstrip that tells about Jeremiah. Some students may have more interest and ability in writing, while others will find that illustrating is their strength. When writing and illustrating are offered as options and the students can work together, the result is a high degree of motivation and involvement, which leads to increased potential for learning.

Audio visuals should never be used as an end in themselves. A good film, filmstrip, recording, or whatever, is most effective when included as an integral part of the lesson plan. To use a resource to fill time, or because a teacher doesn't know what else to do, is to misuse the resource. The resource may be interesting or entertaining, but that is not sufficient reason for using it as part of the teaching process.

Teachers will find that audio visuals are most effective when they are directly related to the main idea and objectives of the lesson plan. The purpose of using an audio-visual resource is to assist the teacher in communicating the main idea of the session, so that the students will be able to accomplish the intended objectives. In order to relate the audio visual to the main idea and objectives, it is imperative that teachers preview the resources so that they can plan activities that lead into use of the audio visual, as well as activities that follow up. To prepare questions, to know when and where to start or turn off the resource, to plan for creative responses to the resource—all require that the teacher take time to become familiar with the resource.

The same is true for practicing with whatever equipment will be used. It is essential that someone be competent and comfortable enough with the equipment to use it without difficulty. There is nothing more frustrating than to have the projector threaded improperly and then have to struggle or wait until the problem is solved. If teachers are uncomfortable in operating an audio-visual device, they should enlist the services of someone who would be willing to assist by operating the equipment.

I realize that many churches have a limited number of audio-visual resources available to them in their own churches. It will take a little extra effort, but there are a number of alternative sources for audio-visual equipment and materials.

1. *Members of the church* often already own slide projectors, cassette recorders, video recorders, and personal computers. There are persons in every church who would be willing to use their equipment with a church school class. (What a marvelous way to recruit an occasional member for a teaching team!)

2. *Neighboring churches,* especially if they are large, may have audio visuals they are willing to loan to others.

3. *Regional church bodies* such as dioceses, presbyteries, associations, districts, conferences, and councils often have one or more resource centers that offer a variety of services. In this day of ecumenical cooperation, teachers will find resource centers of other denominations very willing to share.

82

4. *National rental services* are excellent sources of films and videotapes. There are several rental services listed in the bibliography of this chapter.

There are risks involved in using audio visuals. Most teachers who use them regularly have experienced more than one misfortune. Bulbs can blow out, films can tear or break, machines can malfunction, and any one of a dozen other possible mishaps can cause a well-planned session to go awry. The only way to avoid the risk of misfortune completely is to not use audio visuals at all. Given that alternative, I am more than willing to take the risk. But there are ways to minimize unforeseen problems. Have an extra bulb handy. Set up the equipment carefully and test it ahead of time. Anticipate problems and have altenative strategies in mind. Don't waste time trying to solve problems that are too difficult. And most of all, keep a sense of humor.

When teachers use audio visuals effectively and students respond to them enthusiastically, it is possible to give them more credit than they deserve. Audio visuals are, and will always remain, just inanimate objects. In themselves, they are no more valuable than the use to which they are put by creative teachers who plan carefully and use them effectively. No resource, audio visual or otherwise, will ever become more valuable than the most precious resource present in the classroom—the teacher. It is the teacher who does the planning, the presenting, the asking of questions, the giving of directions, and the inviting of participation. Audio visuals at their best are resources available to assist teachers and students in their teaching and learning.

Possibilities for Using Audio Visuals

The following pages will present brief outlines of suggestions for using five different types of audio visuals. I realize that I could probably write a short book, or at least a whole chapter, on each of the resources. However, in this book, I can only offer some suggestions that will encourage teachers to consider using them. At the end of the chapter I have listed one or more books on each of the audio visuals. These printed resources will be very helpful in providing more information and suggestions.

Photographs

Magazines are the best source of inexpensive photographs: *Life, National Geographic, Newsweek, Time, Sports Illustrated, Smithsonian,* and others. Photographs should be cut out carefully and mounted on a heavier paper—poster board, old file folders, or cover-stock paper. Photographs should be mounted so they will be more permanent and can be used again and again. They can be mounted in several ways:

1. Use rubber cement.

2. Mount with clear contact paper.

3. Use dry-mount press, available from photographers or from teachers' workrooms in schools.

4. Cover the photographs with thin plastic and seal them permanently with a laminating machine.

As I leaf through magazines, I continually watch for photographs that present people of all ages, sizes, and races, and objects or events of all types. I look for pictures that will appeal to the students and invite them to imagine, interpret, and create. I now have a collection of more than two hundred mounted, laminated photographs that can be used for years in a variety of settings—to illustrate songs, hymns and Scripture; to focus on feelings, values, and relationships; to serve as a basis for prayer, conversation, and group building. There are many creative ways to use photographs:

Illustration and Interpretation—From a collection of photographs, each student can select one that expresses for him or her the central meaning of a passage of Scripture or a theological concept. By sharing the reasons for selecting their photographs and telling how they illustrate the meaning of the passage or the concept, the students are able to express their interpretations. The sharing can be done in small groups or with the whole class.

Montage—A montage is a large composite picture composed of a number of smaller, individualized pictures. Students can respond creatively to a biblical passage, a theological

84

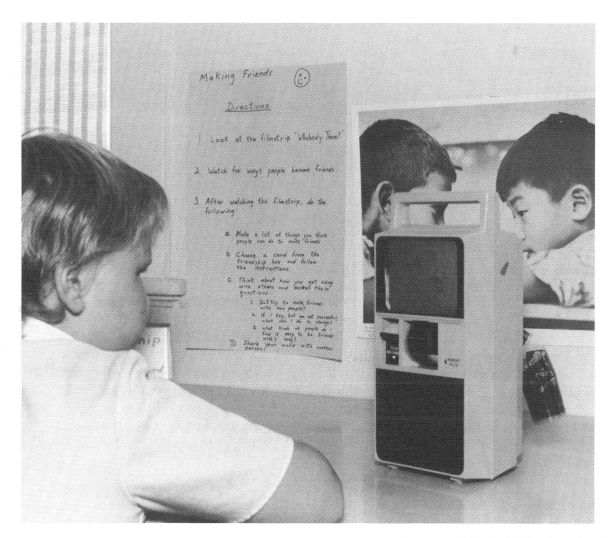

concept, or a social issue by producing a montage. These can be created by individuals or by small groups. The simplest way to construct a montage is to provide a random collection of magazines and allow enough time for the students to find pictures they judge appropriate for illustrating a topic. The pictures may be cut or torn out of the magazines and glued to a sheet of newsprint or poster board.

Or a collection of mounted photographs may be provided. The students choose the appropriate ones, which are then carefully taped or tacked to a bulletin board. If they are taped, small loops of masking tape should be attached to the backs of the photos. If tacked, the head of the tack should overlap the edge of the photo to avoid making a tack hole. Photographs may be used along with traditional teaching pictures to present contrasting visual images in one montage.

Introductions and Group Building—When a new group or class is beginning its life together, persons can introduce themselves to one another by selecting photographs with which they identify, that say something about themselves. They can introduce their pictures (and thus themselves) to two or three others, or perhaps to the whole group if the group is not too large.

85

Storytelling—Every photograph tells a story. There are visual nouns, verbs, adjectives, and adverbs present in good photographs. A photograph can serve as the basis of a story to illustrate feelings, values, relationships, concepts, and so on. Viewers of a photograph can imagine the events that precede and follow the particular visual image. To tell a story, several photographs could be presented in sequence.

Focus for Prayer and Meditation—Each participant is instructed to select one photograph that features two or more persons as the subject. In silent reflection, students are guided by the leader to become intimately acquainted with one of the persons in the photograph: name the person, imagine the person's relationship to others, identify feelings and needs, express concerns and prayers, and respond by offering prayers of intercession, petition, or thanksgiving.

Slides

There are two general categories of slides: photographic slides and do-it-yourself slides. Professionally produced photographic slides can be purchased from collections of museums, tourist attractions, and other commercial agencies. Photographic slides can also be produced by anyone with a 35mm or instamatic camera. Such slides can be candid shots of families, slides of trips and events, and slides of photographs in magazines or books. If the teacher is not experienced with photography, there are probably a dozen or more members of the church who would be more than willing to volunteer their time, expertise, and perhaps even materials to assist in a project involving the production of slides.

"Do it yourself" is my way of describing the process of producing slides without a camera. There are several ways to do it yourself:

Write-On slides are made of an acetate material that can be written or drawn on with pen or pencil. They are designed to be used with transparencies and produce a transparent image. Write-On slides are a Kodak Ektagraphic product, available from audio-visual dealers.

Scratch slides are created by using a sharp instrument to scratch the emulsion off the film of exposed slides, creating a message or illustration. These slides are the result of a photographer's mistake—the lens cap was left on. Most people throw these black slides away. I save them, and even ask the camera store to save them for me.

Picture-lift slides are created by using transparent adhesive plastic or tape. The piece of plastic or tape is placed over a 2 X 2-inch clay-coated magazine picture, adhesive side down. The plastic is rubbed hard with a blunt instrument to "lift" the ink from the picture, transferring it to the adhesive side of the plastic. The plastic and paper "sandwich" is cut out and placed in a container of water to soak the paper from the plastic. The ink with the image remains on the plastic. After rinsing and air drying the piece of plastic, it is mounted on a 2 X 2-inch piece of heavier plastic (the thickness of a slide mount), resulting in a finished slide.

Students can work with slides individually, or cooperatively in small groups:

1. From a collection of photographic slides, select a series to illustrate a song, a hymn, a parable, a psalm, or some other biblical passage.

2. Plan a series of shots to photograph people, events, buildings, or other objects, to create a story or other presentation to share with the class, with other groups in the church, or with the whole congregation.

3. Produce a series of Write-On, scratch, or picture-lift slides to illustrate a passage of Scripture, a hymn, or other subjects.

4. Write a script, captions, or a narration for the slides that have been selected or created.

5. Create one or more slides to graphically illustrate symbols or many dimensions of a key concept.

Filmstrips

Most churches have access to a projector and a variety of filmstrips. Some church school curriculum are accompanied by one or more filmstrips, which may include as few as ten frames or as many as a hundred. Filmstrips with sound narrations are a relatively inexpensive way to combine the visual and audio in one resource. However, filmstrips may be the most misused or underused audio-visual resource in the church. Filmstrips are misused when the teacher uses them just to fill time and does not plan them as an integral part of the teaching strategy. They are also misused when they are expected to carry most of the responsibility for presenting the important information of the lesson, while the students are passive viewers and listeners. Filmstrips are underused in many churches because they are perceived as an old-fashioned, uninteresting resource as compared to movies and television. It is true that filmstrips are a relatively static medium without much action and excitement. However, it may be that what appears as its limitation may, in fact, be its greatest strength. The teacher can control the format and the pace and can involve students with filmstrips in a variety of ways.

Here are twelve different ways to use filmstrips effectively for teaching in the church.

Introduce the subject.—Filmstrips are an effective means for introducing new subjects. Any of several approaches may be used.

1. Instruct the students to look for something specific. When they have a reason for viewing the filmstrip, they will be more observant.

2. The whole class could brainstorm the subject and then view the filmstrip to confirm what they already know and to add new information.

3. Small groups can focus on different questions, so that after seeing the filmstrip the students will be able to participate in a discussion representing more than one perspective.

Present only part of the filmstrip.—When only part of a filmstrip is appropriate to the particular objectives of a class ssession, show only those frames so that the students can focus on that subject.

Use a variety of settings.—It is not necessary that a whole class or group view a filmstrip at the same time. Filmstrips can be used effectively . . .

    . . . in learning centers.

    . . . by small groups exploring or researching a subject.

    . . . by individuals pursuing a particular course of study.

    . . . as a presentation activity for early arrivals.

    . . . as an extra activity for those who finish early.

Prepare your own scripts.—Teachers can use a filmstrip and write their own scripts when . . .

    . . . the script was intended for a different age group.

    . . . the script was inadequate, out of date, or too long.

    . . . the teacher has specific objectives to accomplish.

After students have explored a subject and are familiar with much of the information, give them a filmstrip related to the subject and let them create their own captions or narration for each frame. This activity could be accomplished by individuals as well as small groups.

View a filmstrip without a script.—Teachers could present a filmstrip without the script by asking questions about each frame as it is projected. By responding to the questions, students will be interpreting the visuals through a reflective discussion.

Present the filmstrip twice.—A filmstrip can be used twice in one sitting by presenting it first without a script. Leave each frame on the screen for about twenty seconds, allowing enough time for students to write a one-line caption for the frame. After going through the selected frames this way, the filmstrip can be rewound and shown again so that students can share their captions.

Or a filmstrip can be used first as an introduction and several sessions later as a summary or review.

Set the stage for role-play.—Focus on a person or persons in a filmstrip and stop at a key point, so that students can continue the story line of the filmstrip in a role-play as they identify with one or another character in the story.

Use it in a worship setting.—A filmstrip can be an excellent resource in a worship setting to present a passage of Scripture, a biblical person, or other special theme.

Use multi-media presentations.—Project two filmstrips on the same subject simultaneously. Or project a filmstrip with another medium such as slides, 16mm film, overhead transparencies, or a student-created filmstrip.

Leave filmstrips open-ended.—Instead of showing filmstrips from beginning to end, stop the filmstrip at an appropriate place and lead students in a discussion of possible endings. Or they can create their own endings through role-play, art work, or slide making.

Prepare your own filmstrips.—Using 35mm matte acetate film, students can create their own filmstrips. They could be given a script from a filmstrip, or write their own.

When filmstrips are used creatively in a variety of ways, they will become more interesting. Students tend to be turned off when filmstrips are used only to present information or when they see the filmstrip from beginning to end without being encouraged to become involved. Even old filmstrips can be used creatively if teachers and students use a little imagination.

Cassette Tapes and Recorders

Cassette-tape recorders may be the most available inexpensive audio-visual equipment for church teachers and students. A recorder purchased for as little as $50 will be of sufficient quality for use in any church school classroom. *Cassette* is a French word for *case*. The tape is self-contained in a small case of standard size and can be used interchangeably in any cassette recorder. The recorders are very easy to operate in either the record or playback modes—so easy that even young children can use them successfully.

Blank cassettes and prerecorded cassettes of various types can be used in many creative ways. *Teachers* can use blank tapes in several different ways:

1. On a blank tape, the teacher can record directions for an exploring or creating activity to guide individuals or small groups of students as they work independently. The teacher is then free to work with other students on different activities.

2. Stories, case-study situations, and biblical narratives can be prerecorded to serve as a resource for those who have difficulty reading, or for a learning center.

3. Filmstrip scripts for which there are no recordings, or which need to be revised, can be recorded by the teacher so that the filmstrip can be presented without having someone read the script.

4. Interviews with church staff and officers can be recorded, as well as interviews with others who would have something of value to share with the students.

5. With an inexpensive device, phone calls can be recorded so that it is possible to share conversations with denominational leaders, missionaries at home and abroad, and other prominent persons who otherwise would be unavailable to the church school class. (Caution: Be sure to arrange ahead of time with the persons to be called, and request their permission to record the calls!)

6. Music to accompany the singing of hymns and songs can be prerecorded by a soloist, an organist, or any pianist. With access to a tape recorder, nonmusical teachers should have no excuse for omitting music experiences from the class.

Student-prepared tapes may be even more valuable than other tapes because of the active participation by the students. Some students are not highly motivated to write stories, essays, or dialogues, but might enjoy telling a story or creating a dialogue by speaking into a tape recorder.

1. Scripts for filmstrips, puppet plays, informal dramas, and slide shows can be developed by the students and recorded to accompany the activity.

2. A cassette recorder is a marvelous device for students to use to record interviews with members of the church, asking them questions related to the main idea of the session. Older members can be interviewed about the church's history. Leaders and officers can be interviewed to learn their concerns and insights. Younger students may be more willing to talk with adults in order to record what the adults have to say, than to speak with them at other times.

3. Students can create simulated interviews with biblical characters. One student can act as a radio reporter and the other as the biblical character.

4. Most teachers have family or friends who are members of churches in other parts of the country. Arrangements can be made to exchange tapes with a church school class of the same age group in another church.

Teacher- and student-prepared tapes are the least expensive. One needs only blank tapes, a recorder, and the time to produce the recording. In addition to these home-produced tapes there are commercially produced tapes. Curriculum publishers, music publishers, the American Bible Society, Thesis Cassettes, and many other organizations produce hundreds of different cassette-tape programs that can be used effectively in Christian education.

Overhead Projectors and Transparencies

The overhead projector is one of the most versatile pieces of audio-visual equipment, and its operation can be easily mastered by most teachers. These projectors are relatively inexpensive, and when used effectively the cost is more than justified. There are commercially produced software resources that are quite expensive, but the most effective resources are those the teachers and students can develop themselves from readily available materials.

Overhead projectors are often confused with opaque projectors. An opaque projector is heavy, quite expensive, and must be used in a darkened room. It can project images only from printed material such as books, magazines, and charts. The light is reflected from the original image and enlarged on a screen. But the light in an overhead projector is projected through a transparency inscribed with printed or illustrated images. With the present technology of photocopy machines, it is possible to produce transparencies of just about any printed material a teacher would want to project on a screen. Images can also be produced on transparencies (sheets of clear acetate-plastic) with projection pens or pencils in many colors.

There are many good reasons for considering the use of an overhead projector. A verbal presentation can be accompanied by and illustrated with visual images, enabling the participants to focus more clearly on the teacher's presentation. The overhead projector can be used without darkening the room. Bright, colorful, vivid images capture the attention. Teachers and students can prepare transparencies ahead of time; they can be stored in file folders or notebooks. If the teacher used an overhead projector for no other reason than as an alternative to a chalkboard or newsprint, it would be worth the investment of money and time. The teacher can face the class in presentations accompanied by an overhead projector and can present prepared material much more quickly, as well as control the pace of the presentation.

The disadvantages of an overhead projector are that the materials must be transparent, so that if a graph, chart, map, or other image from a book is to be projected, it must first be reproduced on a transparency by use of a copy machine, or it must be traced by hand. Although it takes time and effort to prepare quality materials, commercially produced transparencies are too expensive for most church budgets.

Blank transparencies, however, cost less than 10¢ each when purchased in quantity, and I am convinced that, as inexpensive as they are, they are much more valuable than those that are commercially produced. With blank transparencies and a pack of color-projection pens, teachers can prepare visual materials specially tailored for a particular class. Also, students can produce marvelous visual images as they express themselves creatively in a variety of ways.

Teacher-prepared transparencies can be of many types and for a variety of purposes:

1. Lists of events, definitions of words, and outlines of topics may be written in one or more colors. (When writing on a transparency, it is best to print the words.)

2. Words of songs and hymns may be written on transparencies and only one verse at a time projected to help the participants sing.

3. Directions for an activity may be presented on a transparency and left illuminated for students to refer to while they are working.

4. In guiding a discussion or a brainstorming process, the teacher can record questions, ideas, or suggestions offered by the participants.

5. A basic map may be accompanied by one or more transparency overlays to illustrate changes in boundaries, journeys of groups or individuals, or the geographic features of a region.

6. By using specially manufactured acetate with a bond-paper copy machine, it is possible to reproduce on transparencies anything that is printed on a page in an atlas, a student's workbook, or any other printed piece. The best way to do this is to make a copy of each page that contains material you want to include on your transparency. Cut out the parts you want and paste them on a sheet of paper, making a composite of exactly what you want included. Then make the transparency from the sheet of paper.

In this way you can add or delete material as well as enlarge or reduce it, if the copy machine has that capability.

Student-prepared overhead transparencies can be used in many different ways as part of exploring and responding activities:

1. Students working in small groups on a task directed by the teacher can prepare a report on a transparency, or on a portion of a transparency, creating a visual report to accompany the verbal presentation. If two or three groups outline their reports on a different portion of separate transparencies, then all the reports can be viewed simultaneously.

2. Blank transparencies can be used like blank sheets of paper—they can be drawn on with projection pens or pencils to illustrate whatever passage of scripture, concept, topic, or issue the students want to communicate with others.

3. Students or teachers can use the stage of the overhead projector as a slide sorter.

4. The projector can be placed behind a large cloth or sheet as the light source for a shadow play or for shadow puppets.

5. Maps, symbols, line drawings, or other original images can be traced from the printed source to create a transparency. The transparency can then be projected and used in that format, or the images can be projected onto a paper, cloth, or other material that has been attached to the wall, and traced again, to produce banners, posters, larger maps, or wall decorations.

6. Litanies, poems, or other verbal expressions can be printed on transparencies by the students to share with others or to involve others in their participation.

HELPFUL BOOKS

About Using Audio Visuals

Fransecky, Robert B., and Debes, John L. *Visual Literacy: A Way to Learn—A Way to Teach.* Association for Educational Communications and Technology, 1972.

Hack, John. *How to Make Audiovisuals.* Revised Edition. Broadman Press, 1979.

Heinich, Robert; Molenda, Michael; and Russell, James D. *Instructional Media and the New Technologies of Instruction.* John Wiley & Sons, 1982.

Holland, Daniel W.; Nickerson, J. Ashton; and Vaughn, Terry. *Using Nonbroadcast Video in the Church.* Judson Press, 1980.

Jensen, Mary, and Jensen, Andrew. *Audiovisual Ideabook for Churches.* Augsburg Publishing House, 1974.

Kemp, Jerrold E. *Planning and Producing Audiovisual Materials.* Fourth Edition. Harper & Row, 1980.

McGuirk, Donn P. *Better Media for Less Money* and *Better Media—Volume Two.* National Education Project, 1972, 1978.

McNulty, Edward N. *Gadgets, Gimmicks and Grace.* Abbey Press, 1976.

Producing Slides and Filmstrips. A Kodak publication available from photographic dealers.

SOURCES OF RESOURCES

Each of the organizations, distributors, and publishers below is an excellent source for obtaining audio-visual resources. Send for a current catalog from each.

Rental Films

Ecu Film, 810 Twelfth Avenue South, Nashville, TN 37203. (800) 251-4091
Mass Media Ministries, 2116 N. Charles St., Baltimore, MD 21218. (201) 727-3270
TeleKETICS films, Franciscan Communication, 1229 S. Santee Street, Los Angeles, CA 90015.
  (213)746-2916
Pyramid Films, P.O. Box 1048, Santa Monica, CA 90406. (800) 421-2304 (Write for: *How to Use Films in the Religious Community* by Garrett Short.)

Filmstrips

Roa's Filmstrips, 6633 W. Howard Street, Niles, IL 60648. (800) 323-9468
John and Mary Harrell, P.O. Box 9006, Berkeley, CA 94709. (415) 525-7167
TeleKETICS (see above)

Audio-Visual and Educational Supplies

Ed-Tech Service, P.O. Box 407, Chatham, NJ 07928. (201) 635-6475
DEMCO, P.O. Box 7488, Madison, WI 53707. (800) 356-8394
Highsmith, P.O. Box 800A, Ft. Atkinson, WI 53538. (800) 558-2110

CHECKLIST FOR TEACHERS

There are several criteria teachers should keep in mind as they select and use audio visuals. These criteria can serve as a check-list when planning or evaluating lesson plans.

1. Does the audio visual assist the teacher in presenting the main idea?

The planning process should move from main idea to the selection of resources. After the main idea is focused and clarified, it is important to consider alternative resources that will help the teacher to effectively communicate the subject of the lesson. If the resource is interesting, engaging, and entertaining, but does not express the main idea clearly, then the resource should be dismissed.

2. Does the audio visual enable the students to accomplish the intended objectives?

The previous paragraph applies also to objectives. After objectives have been established, resources should be selected to help the students accomplish these objectives. Even though they would enjoy a certain audio visual, it may not be appropriate if it does not help them toward achieving the objectives.

3. Is the audio visual appropriate for the age group?

It is important for teachers to look at resources through the eyes of their students to try to determine whether learning will be enhanced by the use of the audio visual. There are times when vocabulary, graphic visuals, inappropriate language, length of time, or other factors will affect an audio visual's appropriateness for a particular age group.

4. Does the audio visual invite students to think, reflect, imagine, create, and express themselves?

If the primary value of an audio visual is its ability to entertain, I would question its use as part of a lesson plan. There is nothing wrong with entertainment per se, but with such limited time for teaching, a resource should engage students in interpretive and expressive activities. The resource should point beyond itself, to concepts, questions, issues, or possibilities worth spending time on.

5. Is the audio visual flexible, adaptable, and versatile?

The most worthwhile resources are those that can be used by more than one class, for more than one session, and for more than one application. It is worth the time and money involved to purchase a resource that can be used in a variety of ways and settings.

6. Is the audio visual worth the price?

Planning for use of audio visuals requires time and energy on the part of the teacher. If the resource needs to be purchased or rented, then it also costs money. As much as possible, teachers should determine ahead of time whether the resource is worth the time, energy, or money required.

Some additional questions for teachers to consider as they work at using audio visuals:

7. What audio-visual resources (equipment and materials) are available to me in the church?

_____

_____

_____

_____

_____

_____

8. What audio visual resources
   do I use most often?—_____
   do I wish were available to me?—_____
   would I like to learn how to use?—_____

9. Do I preview an audio-visual resource and practice with the equipment before presenting it to the students?
   _____always _____mostly _____seldoom_____never

10. Have I encouraged the students to work with and respond to the available audio-visual resources?
    _____often _____occasionally _____not at all

SUGGESTIONS FOR EDUCATION LEADERS

It may be that teachers and leaders do not use audio-visual resources more often because (a) they are not familiar with available equipment and materials, (b) the hardware does not work and needs repairs, or (c) the software is damaged. There are several things education leaders can do to increase the use of audio visuals:

1. Complete these basic administrative tasks periodically.

   Take inventory of all audio-visual equipment and materials.

   Check all equipment to be sure it works properly.

   Check all materials to be sure they are complete and undamaged.

   Prepare a printed directory of all equipment and materials, with brief descriptions of each item.

   Distribute an audio-visual (A-V) directory to all teachers, youth advisors, group leaders, and committee chairpersons.

   Develop a simple system for reserving, circulating, and returning audio-visual resources.

2. Conduct an audio-visual workshop to instruct all teachers in proper operating procedures for each piece of equipment. If a workshop is not feasible, feature one piece of equipment at each of several teachers' meetings: Introduce it and allow time for practice. The more comfortable teachers become in operating the equipment, the more likely they will be to use it.

3. Since so many different people use equipment and it is not feasible to monitor all the uses, a self-instruction guide can be developed. The steps for operating the equipment can be written clearly and succinctly and keyed with colored dots placed on various switches, dials, knobs, or other components. With well-written guidelines, teachers can practice operating the equipment without attending a workshop.

4. Some churches have found it very helpful to recruit a team of volunteers who will operate audio-visual equipment whenever their assistance is needed. This is a job some persons feel more capable of doing than teaching or leading a group. It is especially helpful if the same team of volunteers is able to maintain the equipment in good repair.

5. The above suggestions are focused primarily on audio-visual equipment. It is equally important to assist teachers in their use of audio-visual *materials*. Often a curriculum suggests specific materials such as a film, filmstrip, cassette tape, map, or teaching pictures. Because of limited space in a teacher's manual, not many alternative ways are suggested to use the recommended materials. Through a teachers' briefing session, or even a one-on-one consultation, the resource can be shared with teachers by previewing it, considering its appropriateness for the lesson plan, and exploring ways to utilize it with the students.

6. A resource-sharing meeting can be planned, and it would be especially helpful if teachers of the same age group from several neighboring churches were invited. Each person is asked to bring the following, focused on a particular topic—parables of Jesus, Moses, or Psalms:

One or two key books to use with students.
One favorite filmstrip.
One useful cassette or record.
One special source of resources—a catalog, a periodical, the name of a store, etc.

If six to ten persons each bring four or five resources, just think of the variety that can be shared in a brief time!

7. Another way to help teachers expand their repertoire in the use of one or more specific types of resources (such as overhead transparencies or photographs) is to involve them in brainstorming. In pairs or threes, they spend twenty minutes brainstorming all the possible ways the particular resource could be used, developing a list of ten or more ways. They then select the five best. In turn, each small group shares a suggestion until all the suggestions are shared. With six to ten persons, it is possible to think of as many as thirty different ways to use a particular resource.

Chapter Seven

NURTURING
FAITH

From one perspective it appears that teaching is a very complicated process. Much knowledge and many skills are required in order for the teacher to feel that he or she is doing an effective job. There is a lot to know about the Bible, about theology, education theory, human development, and group process. There are many skills to master in planning lessons, using Bible study tools, guiding interaction, leading instructional activities, and using audio visuals. In the previous six chapters it may seem that I have contributed to the perception that teaching is a complicated process. All this knowledge and these skills are necessary, but that is not the whole picture.

Approaching teaching from another perspective, it appears to be a rather simple process. Teaching in the church is simply sharing the story of God's mighty acts of creating, redeeming, and equipping a people to be the bearers of the good news of love, peace, and justice known most clearly in Jesus Christ. Teaching is sharing—sharing one's own experiences of God, sharing the church's experiences of God, sharing relationships that grow toward friendship, and sharing ideas, feelings, beliefs, and values that reflect what it means to be Christian. From this perspective teachers are quite effective when they enjoy being with others as they give of themselves in interpersonal relationships.

Teaching is not just one or the other of the above descriptions, but *both*. We are mistaken if we approach teaching only as a repertoire of skills used in a process of transmitting important information. Teaching is more than that. We are equally mistaken if we see teaching only as a matter of being with students, enjoying the time together as we share important experiences. Teaching is more than that. Teaching involves skills *and* relationships, information *and* ideas, presenting *and* receiving, as well as structure *and* spontaneity.

Central to the purpose of Christian education is the desire to help persons of all ages to affirm their commitment to Jesus Christ, to know what it means to be Christians, and to live responsibly as Jesus' disciples in the world. It is very difficult, if not impossible, to teach persons to be Christians. We can teach about the Bible, about theology, and about the Christian life. However, as church teachers, we should never fool ourselves into thinking that because we and the students have mastered the subject matter, we have thereby demonstrated our faith and our faithfulness. Faith is not something that can be transmitted to another. It is not something that is learned directly and quickly. Faith is, on the other hand, an aspect of a person's life that emerges from within, is influenced by many tangible and intangible factors and, in the end, is a result of God's work more than the teacher's.

We can teach about Christian beliefs by presenting what other Christians have believed in various periods of the church's history and by sharing our own personal beliefs. And we can invite the students to articulate what they believe. However, teaching about beliefs is not the same as communicating what faith and faithfulness are. Faith is a relationship between a person and God. One does not define faith as a concept as much as one describes faith as an experience. Faith is the response of the whole person in accepting God's gifts of life, of love, of forgiveness, and of salvation through God's Son, Jesus Christ. A person lives in faith, trusting that the good news of the gospel of Jesus Christ is not just good news for the moment but for one's whole life, as well as for the life of the whole world. Living with God in faith and sharing that relationship with others involves one's whole being; faith is an intellectual, emotional, and spiritual affair.

In the Bible the word for *faith* is a key word to describe the relationship between God and persons. The primary characteristics of that relationship are *belief, trust, obedience,* and *hope. Belief* is seen as belief in God or belief in Jesus. It is not a matter of believing what someone else has said or written, but is directed toward the one with whom the relationship has been established.

Trust in God is based upon the memory of what God has done in the past and the experience of what God is doing in the present—to be known to the people, to bring deliverance to the people, and to establish peace and justice throughout the world.

Because of the relationship between God and persons, a relationship established in trust, love, and forgiveness, a person is able to respond in *obedience* to God. In Hebrews, chapter eleven, there appears a litany of people described as having faith and, because of their faith, as having done many great acts in obedience to God.

The fourth dimension of faith is *hope.* In a relationship built upon trust and expressed by obedience, it is possible to have hope for the future. Hope is not a result of mere wishful thinking or of being optimistic, but of having confidence that God's power and presence will be sustained even in a future that appears unpromising.

If a primary goal of Christian education is to help persons grow toward a relationship of faith with God, and yet faith is not something that can be taught directly, what then is the role of the teacher in this process? To understand that role, it is important to understand the difference between instruction and nurture, between direct influence and indirect influence. In the process of instruction the teacher devises teaching strategies that enable students to deal with information and ideas about various aspects of the Christian heritage. Telling stories, asking questions, guiding interaction, encouraging creative expression—all are examples of specific things teachers do to encourage learning. Activities such as these have a direct influence on the learning of the students. It is very important for teachers to develop the skill to use such instructional activities effectively.

Nurture is different from instruction. Comparing instruction to nurture is like comparing a lesson plan to the experience of love and acceptance. The teacher is not only an instructor, but a nurturer. It is not necessary for teachers to compartmentalize activities into instructional and nurturing. But it is necessary for them to realize they are involved in and responsible for more than instruction.

To be satisfied that students have achieved the intended objectives for a particular session, as important as that is, is to be satisfied with too little. Teachers need to enlarge their view of what is happening in the classroom to realize that it is possible, in small and large ways, to be a nurturing influence that provides the students with opportunities to grow in their relationship with God. Of course, teachers are not the only ones who serve in a nurturing role. Family, friends, other teachers, pastors, the congregation, as well as the Holy Spirit—especially the Holy Spirit—all nurture an individual to experience and express faith in God and to live faithfully in that relationship.

Teachers cannot plan lessons to produce faith, and they should not expect that all students will experience faith or express that faith in the same way. Nor should they presume that others are more responsible for nurturing the students in their faith. Teachers can do many specific things to establish an environment, to set the stage, and to plan for learning experiences that have the potential for nurturing students in their own faithful relationships with God. A number of these things have been suggested in earlier chapters. When teachers work at building relationships (Chapter 1), they are preparing the soil in which faith has the opportunity to take root and grow. Encouraging participation and interaction (Chapter 2) creates an environment in which faith can be explored, shared, and nurtured. As they plan for teaching (Chapter 3), especially for exploring and responding activities, teachers are providing occasions in which students can deal with their understandings and experiences of faith. Students who develop skills in studying the Bible (Chapter 4) will have the necessary preparation for encountering the biblical witness to faith and the faithfulness of God's people. When they are enabled to express themselves creatively (Chapter 5), when their creative expressions are accepted and affirmed, they are more likely to risk declaring their faith in God. Even audio visuals (Chapter 6) may influence students to grow in faith, especially when the resources present faith experiences and relationships of biblical, historical, and contemporary people of God.

I have tried to suggest that teaching involves more than being satisfied with a good lesson plan and a happy experience on Sunday morning. Teaching also involves a personal faith relationship with God, an enthusiasm for sharing the good news of Jesus Christ, a desire to be with, care about, and struggle with others, and a willingness to be used by God to nurture others in their faith. By the nature of their relationship with God, with the church, and with their students, teachers are a major influence in setting the stage for encountering God and for growth in a relationship of faith with God. The remainder of this chapter will suggest some specific ways teachers can assist students to grow in their faith.

Teaching Activities That Encourage Growth in Faith

Relate subject matter to personal experiences, needs, and interests.

When deciding whether a subject is appropriate for a particular age group, consider the extent to which the students can relate to the subject on the basis of their own experiences, needs, or interests. If a way cannot be found to connect the subject of the session to the students' own lives, then there might be a question as to whether it is appropriate at that time. At the opening of a session, it is helpful to engage the students in reflecting on and sharing something of their own experiences, even before introducing the biblical passage for the session. Here are some examples:

1. Before presenting the story of Jesus' call of the disciples, the teacher can ask the students to think about important leaders. What makes a good leader? Why would you be willing to follow a leader? What would you want to find out before you decided to follow a leader?

2. Before telling of the time when Peter and John were warned to stop preaching the good news or be put in jail, the teacher could guide students to think about and share times when they have spoken up for things they believed, only to be criticized or perhaps punished.

3. Before discussing the story of Jesus' calming the storm, the students could be asked to think about a time when they were terribly frightened—perhaps even more afraid than they need have been.

After being involved in reflecting on and sharing some of their own experiences, the

102

students will be more motivated to encounter the biblical passage. They will be able to interact with the passage and with one another, out of the context of their own life situations.

It is also possible for students to relate the Bible stories, persons, and events to their own lives in parts of the lesson other than the opening. In Chapter 2 we considered the type of question that invites students to make connections between the subject and their own personal lives. We described these as personalized questions. Whenever a teacher utilizes personalized questions, the students are being asked to reflect on the subject from the frame of reference of their own life experiences.

Teachers can devise other activities that enable the students to build bridges between their own experiences and those of others in their world, and the experiences of individuals and groups among God's people in biblical times.

Encourage persons to share feelings, beliefs, values, and hopes.

One's faith relationship with God is a very personal affair. Faith, as we have already suggested, involves the intellect and the emotions, as well as the spiritual aspects of one's life. It is extremely difficult to explore the meaning of faith, to affirm faith in God, and to share that faith with others, if one has not already had a number of opportunities to reflect upon and speak about feelings, beliefs, values, and hopes. From both the teacher's and the students' perspective, it is much easier to talk about information and ideas than about feelings and beliefs. We are on more comfortable ground when we discuss information and ideas because the reference points are easily identified in terms of what is presented in Bible passages, teacher's manuals, students' books, and other resources. When we discuss feelings and beliefs, we move away from passages, books, and resources and closer to the very personal aspects of our lives.

It seems to me that if we desire to nurture the growing faith of our students, we need to be willing to risk sharing our own feelings, beliefs, values, and hopes, and be open to receiving and responding to the students as they share themselves. I am not suggesting that we abandon our lesson plans and transform the class session into a sensitivity group that involves only personal sharing of feelings. I am suggesting that when we explore passages of scripture, theological concepts, and contemporary issues, we should seek ways to relate our own personal experiences to what we are studying. For instance, if we are focusing on psalms of lament, our study would be incomplete if we did not encourage persons to speak or write their own laments that they would express to God. If we are exploring the prophet Amos and focusing on the injustices he exposed, our study would be enriched by encouraging the students to share some of their responses to the injustices that are present in our own society. If we are working with the passage in which Jesus asks, "Who do men say that I am?" and after several responses asks the disciples directly, "Who do you say I am?" the study would not be complete without also asking the students to express their answers to the question, "Who do you believe Jesus to be?"

These illustrations suggest that the teacher needs to move the study to a more personal level by inviting the students to express their own personal feelings, beliefs, values, and hopes. Curriculum resources often lack this dimension, so teachers need to take the initiative to be sure it happens. It is important not to pressure the students so that they feel embarrassed. We want them to speak from their own personal experiences, but we do not want the discussion to become so personal that they feel self-conscious to the point of embarrassment.

When we encourage students to share their feelings and beliefs, there are several guidelines we teachers need to keep in mind.

1. Never put persons on the spot by calling on them before they are ready to speak. Instead, ask the question and offer an invitation to the whole group, then wait the necessary time (5-15 seconds) for someone to respond.

2. When someone does share personal feelings or beliefs, listen attentively and accept what the person says, even though you do not agree. Be supportive and affirming of the person, even if you cannot affirm what the person has said.

3. Ideas, theories, and interpretations can be debated, but personal feelings, beliefs, values, and hopes are not subjects for debate. It is important to distinguish the difference and to encourage the participants to realize the difference. To debate someone's feelings would be to deny the person the right to have those feelings, and that person, as well as others, would soon be unwilling to share personal feelings.

4. As teachers, who model the whole process for the students, we need to be willing to share our feelings and beliefs as well as asking the students to share theirs. We share so as not to suggest we have the only correct way of responding, but rather that we are partners with the students in the process of learning and growing.

By encouraging students to share their feelings, beliefs, values, and hopes as a normal part of the learning process, it may become easier for them to affirm their faith in Jesus Christ as their Lord and Savior and to witness to that faith in settings other than the church classroom. If in the church school persons only study about their faith and are never encouraged to witness to that faith, then we should not be surprised at their reluctance to share their faith with others outside the church classroom.

Identify with biblical events, persons, and issues.

Teachers can be very intentional in their planning to devise activities that encourage students to identify with events and persons in the Bible. Through role-play, imagination, or creative writing, the students speak, think, or write as if they are the biblical persons. For instance, if the lesson is dealing with Jesus' crucifixion and the disciples' response to that terrible event, the teacher can set the stage by saying something like this:

Let's put ourselves in the place of the disciples. Let's put their sandals on our feet. Let's try to think and feel and speak as the disciples might have on the day after Jesus' crucifixion. Today is Saturday. Yesterday our teacher and Lord was crucified. As we are huddled together in the home of a friend, the only question on our minds is, "What are we going to do now? Now that Jesus is dead, what do we do next?" Let's talk about it as the disciples might have talked.

As the students speak in a role-play format, imagining they are the disciples, they will begin to express ideas and feelings, but without realizing it, they will be sharing their own ideas and feelings.

When I was teaching a group of fifth- and sixth-graders, we worked in a learning center format. One of the centers directed the students to listen to a recording of a dramatization of Jesus calling Matthew to be a disciple. One of the possible responding activities was to create a reporter's interview of Matthew. Two fifth-graders spent most of the session in that learning center, working together to create an interview which they recorded to share with the rest of the class. I remember that the reporter (David) asked Matthew (Libby), "Why did you decide to follow Jesus?" Matthew (Libby) answered, "Because I wanted to be with him. I knew he was right in what he said. And besides, I really love Jesus." I have a hunch that Libby will be more able to say for herself, "I really love Jesus," because she was able to express those words in a nurturing, supportive activity and setting.

Students need opportunities week by week to use their imagination to identify with biblical events and persons. Through role-play, informal dramatics, puppet plays, creative writing, and simulation games, students can be involved in activities that contribute to their getting in touch with the faith experiences and relationships of others. As they identify with those faith experiences, they are helped to grow in their own faith. I have emphasized biblical events and persons, but the same principles would apply to historical and contemporary events and persons.

As teachers seek to involve students in these activities, there are several principles that should be kept in mind.

1. Before students can be successful in identifying with events and persons from another time-frame, it is important to have sufficient background information, or the role-playing, speaking, and writing will be unfocused and unproductive. This information can be provided by telling a story, viewing a filmstrip, exploring resources, or other appropriate presenting and exploring activities.

2. In addition to setting the stage with information, teachers need to provide clear, concise directions to help the students know what is expected of them and to provide smooth movement from one step of the activity to the next. The teacher may have clearly in mind what is expected of the students, but should never presume that it is equally clear to the students. Clear, concise directions are an essential prerequisite for a successful activity.

3. After experiencing a role-play, a simulation game, creative writing, or other activity, it is very important to take time to reflect on that experience. It is one thing to identify with and speak in the role of Moses, and it is something quite different to reflect upon and speak about the experience, and then to extend the discussion to include present, personal feelings, beliefs, and values.

Write and share prayers and statements of belief.

When I was in the seventh grade, my church school teacher expected each member of the class to offer a sentence prayer every week. The prayers were supposed to be spontaneous, around the circle. This was a brand new experience for me, and what I remember most was being uncomfortable, embarrassed, and tongue-tied. I could never think of a thing to pray about, and whatever I said seemed silly. I have talked with others who recall similar experiences.

During my senior year in high school, my family moved from New Jersey to California. Shortly after arriving in my new town, I went to the youth fellowship group at church. I remember clearly, and painfully, one meeting when I was called upon by the leader to give "a testimony to my Christian faith." I had never been asked to do such a thing before. I was the "new kid in town," and I was completely unprepared. I haven't the slightest recollection of what I said, but I do recall feeling confused, embarrassed, and intensely self-conscious. When I have shared this with others, they have identified similar experiences in their own lives.

There is nothing wrong with inviting students to pray and to speak about their faith. In fact, I think it is one of the key tasks of teachers to guide students to be able to pray in a group and to share their Christian beliefs with others. It is possible that as students are encouraged to pray and express what they believe, teachers may be doing more to nurture their faith than in any other activity. One's experience and understanding of faith may be better expressed in prayers and statements of belief than in any other way. However, there are ways teachers can be more helpful and nurturing than in the two personal experiences I have described. Fotunately, there were sufficient positive experiences with teachers and my fellow students in that seventh-grade Sunday school class and in that youth fellowship to overshadow the two negative experiences.

Instead of using sentence prayers in a circle as an opening or closing ritual, teachers would be more helpful in teaching about prayer and encouraging students to pray if they kept some important guidelines in mind.

1. First, students need to learn about prayer: types of prayers, the language of prayer, reasons for praying, and examples of prayers.

2. After learning about prayer, there should be opportunities to read good examples—prayers of authors, ministers, the psalmists, and others—and to pray in unison as a group, as well as aloud individually.

3. Instead of expecting students to pray extemporaneously, time should be given to think about or to write down their prayers so they will be more comfortable while speaking.

4. Instead of going around in a circle, where all the students feel put on the spot and do not hear any of the other prayers because they are so preoccupied with their own words, it would be much more appropriate to make praying aloud optional.

5. Instead of calling upon members of the class to pray extemporaneously, ask them ahead of time so they can be prepared.

6. Encourage persons to select portions of the psalms or other prayers of the masters and read them aloud, instead of having to make up their own.

7. Litanies can be created quickly by teachers and students. Focus the students' attention on a particular concern, theme, or concept, such as, "Let us pray for peace in our lives and in the world." Invite them to write sentence prayers for peace, and provide time to do the writing. The teacher prepares a response such as, "O God, hear our prayers for peace." Students can share the prayer statements they have written, one at a time, and the whole group can respond to each one with the litany response.

With careful preparation and sensitivity to the students illustrated by the above guidelines, teachers will be much more supportive and nurturing of the students than by functioning as my seventh-grade church school teacher did.

At the time of confirmation, or becoming a member of a church, persons are usually expected to be able to articulate to some extent what they believe. In many church school lessons and Sunday sermons, there is encouragement to witness to our faith, to share with others what it means to be Christians. The process of stating their beliefs or witnessing to others about their faith is not natural and easy for many people. It is especially difficult to speak about one's faith when there have not been occasions to do so within the affirming, nuturing environment of the classes and groups of which persons are a part in the ongoing life of the church. There are many ways to provide opportunities for students to work at expressing what they believe. Teachers can ask questions that encourage students to express their beliefs:

We have been studying about the various names and titles of Jesus. Which name or title of Jesus expresses what you believe about Jesus?

If someone who had never heard about Jesus approached you and asked who he is, what would your response be?

The Bible is called the Word of God. What does it mean to you to speak of the Bible as the Word of God?

Some people say you can believe in God and worship God without belonging to a church. What do you think about that?

These are just four of the hundreds of possibile questions that will elicit from the participants their own personal expressions of faith. By discussing questions such as these week by week in the church school setting, students will feel better equipped to talk about their beliefs in other settings. Such questions do not presume specific, correct answers. The wider the variety of responses among the students, the more productive the discussion will be. By hearing what others think about a particular subject, a person is better able to clarify personal thoughts and beliefs.

Teachers can plan activities that give students the option to write or speak about their beliefs. For some, a few sentences will be sufficient, whereas others will want to write paragraphs and pages to express themselves. The writing can be in any of several forms, such as the eight examples presented in Chapter 5. Thoughts and beliefs can be spoken in the context of discussions, role-playing, or simulation activities. Whether written or spoken, it is important that students receive feedback from the teacher and other students, but never in the form of criticism or ridicule, which would cause the students to hesitate to share their thoughts and beliefs on another occasion. The feedback should show respect and appreciation for the person as well as for what the person has shared. It is all right to have differences of opinion and to ask questions, but even that kind of feedback can be offered in ways that affirm the person.

In this chapter, as well as in the other six, I have tried to affirm the importance of the teacher's role in nurturing persons to grow in faith and to live faithfully as God's people. This ministry of teaching is necessary in the life of the church. In the week-by-week routine, there are times when teachers wonder whether their work will have any lasting effect. Is it possible to accomplish anything when students attend irregularly and often appear uninterested when they do attend? Yes, there are many times when teaching in the church is a discouraging, unrewarding experience. However, most teachers will report that there are many, many times when a student's insightful comment, challenging question, creative expression, exciting discovery, or joyful smile is evidence enough that all the time and energy spent are truly worth the effort. Teachers are among the most effective resources available to God for reaching out in love to others. Teachers are blessed in their ministry. Teachers are also a blessing to those they teach.

Perhaps the best way to close this chapter and the whole book is to include "A Teacher's Litany of Praise and Thanksgiving."

A TEACHER'S LITANY OF PRAISE AND THANKSGIVING

For the gift of yourself to the whole world and to me;
I give you praise and thanks, O God.

For revealing yourself to me through the words of Holy Scripture;
I give you praise and thanks, O God.

For demonstrating so clearly your love in the life, death, and resurrection of Jesus Christ, your Son and my Saviour;
I give you praise and thanks, O God.

For naming me your child and including me among your people;
I give you praise and thanks, O God.

For calling me to serve in the ministry of teaching;
I give you praise and thanks, O God.

For giving me a story to tell and a faith to share;
I give you praise and thanks, O God.

For providing students with such a variety of gifts, needs, and interests;
I give you praise and thanks, O God.

For equipping me to be their teacher;
I give you praise and thanks, O God.

For the vision of a world that loves you and lives in peace;
I give you praise and thanks, O God.

And for the special opportunity you give to me to serve you and your children as a teacher;
I give myself in obedience to you, with praise and thanks, O God.

Amen!

CHECKLIST FOR TEACHERS

1. What distinctions do I make between instruction and nurture?

   _____
   _____
   _____
   _____
   _____

2. How would I describe my faith relationship with God?

   _____
   _____
   _____
   _____

3. In sharing my own faith story with the students, do I . . .
   _____hesitate to share my beliefs and experiences?
   _____share my experiences when asked?
   _____take every opportunity to speak about my faith?
   _____invite others to share their faith, and listen to them when they do?
   _____expect others to have experiences similar to mine?

4. What are my desires or goals in nurturing the faith of the students?

   _____
   _____
   _____
   _____

5. How often do I relate the subject matter to the personal experiences, needs, and interests of the students?
   _____every session   _____as often as possible
   _____occasionally   _____never

6. Do I encourage students to share their feelings, beliefs, values, and hopes?
   _____most of the time   _____when it is appropriate   _____seldom

7. In planning activities that involve students in identifying with biblical events, persons, and issues, I find that . . .
   _____the curriculum is not very helpful.
   _____I have a hard time devising such activities.
   _____when I do use such activities, the students "come alive."

8. To help students with praying, I . . .
   _____have shared what it means to pray.
   _____shared examples of various types of prayers.
   _____have set an example by praying with them.

_____give them time to think or write what they will pray.
_____invite them to offer their prayers voluntarily.

9. To what extent do I encourage students to express their beliefs in verbal or written form?
   _____every session   _____as often as possible
   _____occasionally   _____never

SUGGESTIONS FOR EDUCATION LEADERS

1. Invite a church educator, pastor, professor, or someone else who is qualified, to speak at a worship service, teacher recognition dinner, or other special event. The topic of the presentation would be "Nurturing Faith," "Growing in Faith," or "Instruction and Nurture."

2. At a regular teachers' meeting, in team planning sessions, or as a part of a one-to-one conversation, the topic "Nurturing Faith" would be a good focus for a discussion. Prior to the discussion everyone can read this chapter which would serve as good stimulus.

3. When recruiting teachers, set aside part of the interview for the prospective teacher to share something of his or her own faith story. The teacher should not be put on the spot and made to feel as if he or she were being examined, but it should be a time of mutual sharing. The recruiter should be willing to share in a personal way also. The teacher can be helped to feel that part of the role of the teacher is to encourage students to share their feelings, beliefs, values, and hopes, so that in the process they will become comfortable in sharing their own faith stories.

HELPFUL BOOKS

About Nurturing Faith

Everist, Norma J. *Education Ministry in the Congregation.* Augsburg Publishing House, 1983.
Foster, Charles R. *Teaching in the Community of Faith.* Abingdon Press, 1982.
Fowler, James W. *Stages of Faith.* Harper & Row, 1981.
Fynn. *Mister God, This Is Anna.* Holt, Rinehart & Winston, 1974.
Little, Sara. *To Set One's Heart.* John Knox Press, 1983.
Nelson, C. Ellis. *Where Faith Begins.* John Knox Press, 1967.
Ng, David, and Thomas, Virginia. *Children in the Worshiping Community.* John Knox Press, 1981.
Rood, Wayne R. *On Nurturing Christians.* Abingdon Press, 1972.
Sherrill, Lewis Joseph. *The Struggle of the Soul.* Macmillan Publishing Co., 1951.
Westerhoff, John H. III. *Will Our Children Have Faith?* Seabury Press, 1976.